ARKEL ANNIVERSARY ALBUM

BY KHADIJA BUCKLAND

With contributions by David Backhouse

A Red House Publication
Printed in Great Britain
by Manor Printing Services

CONTENTS

Published by Red House Publishing ISBN 0-9522519-0-6

WHEN the idea for this book was first mentioned to me, I wasn't sure whether anyone would be interested in an historical work.

But the Arkell's Anniversary Album hasn't turned out to be a corporate history or even just a factual account of a company that has reached the important landmark of 150 years in brewing.

It really reflects what Arkell's is about - family. Not just my own, but the many generations of families that have worked here and made Arkell's what it is today: the longest surviving business in Swindon and also the happiest.

For me this book has stirred up many happy memories - not only of dedicated staff and first-rate licensees that have come and gone but also, in many cases their children who have taken their place. Looking at the old photographs has also made me wonder where the years have gone.

This book traces the growth of Arkell's; from my great – grandfather John and his first pub, to the thriving estate we own today.

It also allows a glimpse into the world of brewing at our Kingsdown Brewery and shows the care and attention that go into every pint. There are full details of many of our beers, past and present, and the stories of our last three Head Brewers.

The families that have formed the backbone of our company are the subject of a chapter as is the bottling plant that at one time brought us great success. And the highlights of the anniversary year and the growth of our wines and spirits division, John Arkell Vintners are also recorded.

The loyalty of our customers has also played a vital part in our success. Without them we would not be celebrating this anniversary. I hope they get as much pleasure out of reading the Arkell's Anniversary Album as I have.

At Arkell's we pride ourselves on staying true to the traditions the company was built on. Many things have changed since 1843, but these haven't.

And that's something we can all drink to!

Peter Arkell Chairman

3

CHAPTER ONE

FROM HOME BREWED
TO COMMERCIAL SUCCESS

A history of Arkell's from 1843 to the present day.

Contributions from David Backhouse

THE HISTORY of Arkell's Brewery is a story not just of one company or even one family. It is about the foresight and determination of individuals, of how social change can create opportunities and how a business that stays loyal to its founding traditions can succeed.

The Brewery's founder John Arkell was born to a farming family in Kempsford, South Gloucestershire, in 1802. Agriculture was undergoing hard times in the early 18th century so in 1830 John and his cousin Thomas decided to emigrate to the New World, taking a party of local people with them.

After travelling through America they arrived in Canada. There they established the village of Arkell which today is a thriving community and still bears the family name. However, John decided to return home in 1833. He married and settled down to farm several miles away from his family

John Arkell
1801 - 1881

home at Stratton in Wiltshire.

John grew barley in his fields and it made business sense to start brewing beer. There were already several commercial breweries in the area, serving mainly the local market towns. But many pubs still brewed their own beer just as they had done for centuries. The Brewery was established as an offshoot of the farm in 1843. A better location or time to open a brewery could hardly have been found. Brunel had recently chosen open land between Stratton and nearby Swindon – then little more than a hilltop market town – as the site of his main locomotives and carriage works for the Great Western Railway.

Within a few years New Swindon had grown into a sizeable town, populated almost entirely by GWR employees. After toiling in the massive workshops these men needed

4

A view of the Brewery taken by Mr Hooper, a local photographer, c.1900.
His tricycle is in the foreground.

refreshment. Hardly surprisingly the number of beerhouses in the area mushroomed.

John Arkell had a ready-made local market for his beer. Swindon had become a boom town and his beer production expanded rapidly, despite fierce competition from rival breweries.

But Arkell's beer was becoming a firm favourite in Swindon and production was stepped up. In 1856 the Swindon Advertiser printed "Mr John Arkell invited his friends to dine in his new 3,000 gallon barrel; the novel dining room was the scene of much mirth and gaiety."

Nevertheless, demand soon outstripped the capacity of the existing plant and in 1861 a new brewery was built nearby at Kingsdown on land behind the original Kingsdown Inn.

Even this new brewery was not enough to cope with the growing demand and it was extended after just six years. A new Kingsdown Inn was built across the road and the original pub turned into the brewery offices which are still used today. A large maltings was erected in 1877 by which time rapid expansion of the brewery's tied estate was underway through the acquisition of pubs within a 15 mile radius.

By this time John had taken his eldest son Thomas into partnership, to be followed later by his youngest son, James.

For his whole life John Arkell espoused the Liberal cause and became well known in the area for his views, even though these sometimes brought him up against the establishment. It was reported many years later that the local Tory magistrates would not grant a licence for his first public house and he had to appeal to the Quarter Sessions to obtain it.

Graham Arkell

The company was built on solid foundations and John became known as 'Honest John'. As a business it made steady, if unspectacular progress acquiring pubs here and there as they came onto the market and, from 1870, building new ones in expanding New Swindon.

John Arkell died peacefully at the Malt House, Stratton, on 21 October 1881. The Swindon Advertiser reported that shops were closed and window blinds drawn as the funeral cortege passed on its way to Stratton Church. "He was open and above board and Radical in all he said and did. The poor had lost a good friend, a plain and simple friend," said the paper.

He was succeeded by his sons Thomas and

Sir Noël Arkell

He wrote many letters that were published in the Swindon Advertiser and made long speeches at political functions. During one lengthy address at the Mechanics Institute, the building in Swindon's Railway Village opened by the GWR for the education of its workers, it is said that he was constantly interrupted by the caretaker calling 'time'.

Unlike many other local brewers, it seems little attempt was made to woo the free trade. In 20 years of Swindon newspapers there are only a couple of advertisements for Kingsdown Ales.

One of these in 1860 announced: "4X 1s.8d - 2s.0d, 3X 1s.4d - 1s.6d, XX 1s.0d - 1s.2d, X 8d - 10d, and Table Ale 6d a gallon".

Oliver Arkell

The Rampant Cat. In 1897, when the magistrates demanded that the pub be closed in order to provide a licence for the new County Ground Hotel in Swindon, James lost no time in shutting The Rampant Cat!

Thomas died in 1919 at the ripe old age of 80 and James, aged 75, in 1925. The business passed to James's sons Thomas Noël (later Sir Noël), James Graham and John Oliver Arkell. It became a private limited company in 1927, all shares being taken by members of the family. Today all the shares are still owned by the family.

The brewing book of this period shows four beers being produced at Kingsdown: Mild (bottled as Home-Brewed) original gravity 1039, BB (bottled as Pale Ale) o.g. also 1039, Stout o.g. 1042 and BBB o.g. 1054.

The Kingsdown Brewery, which by that time had operated for nearly 70 years with little alteration, now began to be modernised. The maltings were closed in the 1930's and a new bottling store installed in the building in 1937. In its heyday this employed some 25 people – mainly women, and filled

James. They continued the expansion of the company mainly by buying up pubs thrown onto the market when rival breweries went under.

By the turn of the century Arkell's had grown into the largest single owner of pubs in the area, with some 44 in Swindon and North Wiltshire – more than a quarter of the total.

Although an astute businessman, James appeared to be a man who would bear a grudge. He lived at Redlands, Highworth, and was annoyed by the noisy conduct of a nearby Arkell beerhouse,

An Arkell's dray c.1900.

The town of Arkell still exists today on the site where John and the group from Kempsford founded it. It is a small town with a population of 120 just outside the town of Guelph in Ontario around 30 miles from Toronto and 55 miles from the US - Canadian border at Niagara Falls.

1,440 bottles of beer an hour using equipment which was seen at the time as among the most hi-tech in the country.

A couple of years later, a mineral water plant was opened in the Brewery and the production of the Ace soft drinks brand which was to became very much part of the Swindon scene started. Also dating from this period is the tall Brewery chimney.

The tied estate was not ignored between the wars, although a ban on new licences in Swindon meant few new pubs were opened. Instead, a general programme of pub modernisation and refurbishment took place.

After World War Two, redevelopment in central Swindon forced the closure of several pubs. As these closed the licences were transferred to new estate pubs on the outskirts of town.

In the 1960s Arkell's took its first step into the wine and spirits market when it bought Brown & Plummer's, a wine merchants owned by a cousin of the family, in Swindon's Old Town.

By this time Peter Arkell, the eldest son of Sir Noël, was a director and had his own views on how the company should develop.

Peter was born in 1923. He was studying at Oxford when war broke out and he went to fly with the Royal Air Force in England and in Burma. After a serious crash behind enemy lines, he spent a year in hospital before being invalided out of the service.

He tried to resume his degree at Edinburgh University after the War but found the gap in his studies had been too great. Instead he went to Hammond's Brewery in Yorkshire. This company was taken over by the Tadcaster Tower Brewery, where he became a director.

In 1954 he was called to join the family business as a director and became Chairman in 1971. Graham Arkell died in 1972 and Sir Noël in 1981.

A trade exhibition, 1950.

The board of Directors, 1962
Left to right : Sir Noël, Peter and
Graham Arkell Chairman.

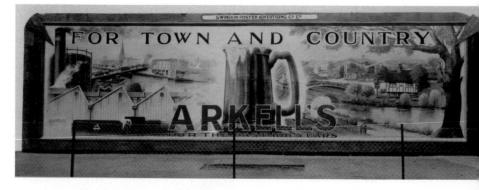

An Arkell's hoarding, early 1960s.

Peter's son James was born in 1951 and on leaving school spent a year ranching in Argentina. He came to Kingsdown in 1970 and then left for various spells of training. These comprised of six months with his second cousin Claude Arkell at his Donnington Brewery near Stow-on-the-Wold, then a spell with Baird's the maltsters, followed by a year studying pub management with Bass.

He became a director in 1973 and a member of the main board in 1974. A second cousin, Nicholas, joined the company in 1973, became a director in 1978 and is now Sales and Vintners Director.

Arkell's venture into wines and spirits was followed by further diversification. In 1967, Austin Amusements was set up as a joint venture, with Derek Austin operating amusement machines in pubs. It now runs hand-in-hand with electrical contractors Austin's Electrical.

Arkell's also holds a 50 per cent interest in Edmont's Joinery, a company employing 70 people, founded in 1972 by Les Clark and Tom Chick. Mr Chick sold his share to Arkell's in

1979. James Arkell is a director together with Mr Clark and Peter Jenkinson, who is married to James's sister, Alison.

Edmont's carries out much of the refurbishment work on Arkell's pubs and is also building contractors, manufacturing joiners, upholsterers and electricians. The company is also shopfitters to well known High Street stores and has undertaken work in airports.

The 1960s saw further changes at the Brewery. The introduction of metal casks in 1960 gradually made the wooden version redundant and the cooper's shop closed in 1968. Also, the promotion of nationally advertised brands of soft drinks forced the reluctant closure of the mineral plant in 1962. The building is now used to house John Arkell Vintners, the wines and spirits department which grew from the acquisition of Brown & Plummer's. The Vintners has expanded rapidly and now has an enviable reputation as the most respected wine merchant in the area.

The tied estate continued to grow, with occasional acquisitions until 1991, when

10

An Arkell's hoarding -
anniversary year, 1993.

James Arkell pulls the first pint at the Adam and Eve,
Gloucestershire, with the Gassons.

Arkell's bought a package of eight Whitbread pubs in Gloucestershire as part of the national firm's disposal programme.

At the same time, the free trade was being extended mainly along the Thames Valley and into London. For the first time in its history, Arkell's beer was being bought and enjoyed in large quantities outside its traditional Swindon and South Gloucestershire heartland.

However, it was not all expansion during this period. The decline in popularity of beer in returnable bottles meant it was found necessary to wind down and finally close the bottling store in 1983. Arkell's beer is now bottled and canned on a contract basis.

But the bottling store closure was only a minor setback in Arkell's expansion at this time and, in 1993, the firm celebrated its 150th anniversary, making it the Swindon area's longest surviving company.

Three generations of Arkells celebrate cask washer Bill Pewsey's 20 years with the company. Left to right : Peter Arkell, James Arkell, Bill Pewsey and Sir Noël Arkell.

11

CHAPTER TWO

BUTCHERS, BAKERS AND MOONRAKERS

Arkells pubs, past and present.

The Kingsdown Inn, Upper Stratton.

WHEN John Arkell brewed his first pint in 1843, nearly half of Britain's pubs produced their own beer. But commercial brewers like Arkell's were keen to buy up pubs and secure a reliable market for their products.

In this way the modern tied estate was born, guaranteeing breweries an outlet for their beer.

From its very beginnings Arkell's realised the importance of owning tied houses around its brewery. Under John Arkell, the foundation of the Brewery's thriving estate of pubs was built. At first several pubs were held on short-term lease but as the company expanded, freeholds were acquired.

The first recorded acquisition was, aptly, The Kingsdown Inn – the brewery tap. The land was bought in 1840 and the original inn erected as a beerhouse with a full licence not granted until 1847. Twenty years later when the Kingsdown Brewery was extended, the original building was needed for offices so a new pub was built across the road with the same name.

12

The George Hotel, Kempsford.

In 1856, Arkell's made its first venture into Swindon. It leased The Carriers Arms in Cricklade Street, Old Town - a beer and lodging house enjoying not the best of reputations. It had been built nine years earlier by one Elijah Rushan although research shows it may have replaced a beerhouse originally on the site.

Even a change of name to The Lord Raglan, after the Crimean War hero, could not save its reputation and the local constabulary were regular critics. The pub seems to have been frequented mainly by down and outs.

Advertisements of the time describe the pub as being an agent for Kingsdown Brewery Ales and Porter and offering "Ales and Porter of first quality". George Trout, landlord, also offered 2s 6d per dozen for rabbit skins,

according to an 1867 advertisement.

This advertisement also boasts "well-aired beds". As other advertisements of the time put the number of beds at 40, they must have also been well used – the 1871 Census shows no less than 56 people occupying them, including an entire German band!

Arkell's acquired the pub outright in 1889 but it was closed by the magistrates in 1907. The building was not demolished until 1981 to make way for offices.

John Arkell returned to his home village of Kempsford for his third pub, buying The George in 1861. Over the next ten years the Brewery went on a spending spree, buying pubs around Swindon and Cirencester and setting in place the pattern for the future tied estate.

13

The Fox in Highworth was bought at an auction in 1862 after the bankruptcy of H. St. John Medley, a brewer of Faringdon. This was followed by The Harrow in Wanborough, which was taken on a ten-year lease.

The Golden Cross in Cirencester was bought in 1864 followed at around the same time by Arkell's second pub in Swindon - this time in the new town's main shopping street. The Artillery Arms in Regent Street, Swindon, survived until 1936 when it was closed and demolished to enable the building of a Woolworth's store. In its latter days it is said that it enjoyed a particularly rowdy reputation.

The Tavern in Greatfield was bought in 1866, later renamed The Butchers Arms. The Plough in Devizes Road, Swindon, was added a year later and The Crown at Stratton in 1868.

In 1869 the estate was expanded by three pubs: The Brewers Arms in Cirencester, the Eight Bells at Fairford and The Duke of Wellington in Eastcott Hill, Swindon.

This last pub was modified from a pair of newly-built terraced houses and was opened in a rush before the repeal of the Beerhouse Act of 1830.

This Act had allowed any householder to open as a beerhouse, free from a magistrates' licence on payment of two guineas. John Arkell bought the houses on 30 March and the pub was open by the October when the new law came in. As it was already open, the licensing magistrates had no choice but to allow it to stay open. John Arkell must have had a wry sense of humour — the Beerhouse Act's original author was the Duke of Wellington!

Rapid expansion continued, despite licensing changes, with The Bakers Arms in Faringdon and The Wheatsheaf in Ermin Street, Stratton, added in 1870. The latter had been let to the Star Brewery of Stratton at a weekly rental of 1s.0d (5p)!

This year also saw the first purpose-built Arkell's pub in Swindon, The Great Western, opposite the railway station. The original licence application was supported by the station porters who complained that the nearby Queens Tap was overcharging for its beer at 2d a pint.

A large wing of residential bedrooms was added in 1904. By 1973, lettings had ceased and the

The Great Western Hotel late 1950s - now called the Flag and Whistle.

These cartoon ads used to appear on the back of Swindon Town FC's fixture lists during the 1960s and 1970s

The Dophin Hotel - built by Arkell's in 1873.

The Duke of Edinburgh, also built by the Brewery in 1873.

whole building became a pub-restaurant called The Noah's Ark. The name reverted to the original in 1983 but, after further refurbishment in 1991, the premises are now known as the Flag and Whistle.

In 1871, The Plume of Feathers in Cirencester was bought and in 1872 The Wild Deer in Swindon. The Brewers Arms in Wanborough, originally a brewery owned and operated by one Thomas Turtle, was added in the following year.

Two new pubs were built in Swindon this year, The Dolphin and The Duke of Edinburgh, strengthening the company's foothold in the rapidly expanding town.

The Dolphin had a licence granted on

'Trip' Saturdays when virtually the whole town left by special trains for the seaside. This licence allowed it to open from 4am to 6am and must have added to the jollity of departing holidaymakers.

The Duke of Edinburgh had operated from small premises nearby called The Tabernacle or Halfway House. These were replaced by a new building which cost £1,200 to build.

The Red Lion at Lechlade was bought in 1874 followed by The White Hart at Moredon in 1875, The Borough Arms, Wootton Bassett in 1876 and, in 1877, The Talbot in Cirencester and The Red Lion at Moredon which was immediately replaced by a new building adjoining the original; The White Hart, which lay opposite, was closed.

Its licence was transferred to another new Arkell's house, The Mechanics Arms in Cheltenham Street, near Swindon's town centre. This pub closed and was demolished to make way for the bus station in 1961, only a year after it was granted a full licence.

Another pub which would eventually succumb to the town planners was The Carpenters Arms in Cricklade Road, Swindon, bought in 1877. This had been an off-licence and lasted as a pub until 1964 when it was demolished to enable road widening.

The following year, The Belle Vue Inn and brewery in Swindon were bought. The brewery was immediately closed and at some later date turned into the pub now known as Longs Bar. The original pub, which lay at the rear in Belle Vue Road, was put to various uses, but now has been incorporated into Longs Bar.

Longs Bar as it used to look - pre 1960s.

16

The Carpenters Arms, Gorse Hill c.1959 (demolished in 1964).

e Mechanics
s, late 1950s
molished to
ake way for
vindon Bus
on in 1961).

17

The Lamb and Flag
early 1960s.

The Mason's Arms
(demolished in 1969).

The White Hart, Stratton St. Margaret c.1900
Licensee Mr James stands outside with some of his regulars.

In 1878 The White Hart at Stratton was acquired, followed in 1879 by The Fox and Hounds, Wroughton.

The New Inn in Cromwell Street, Swindon, was bought in 1880 although this too was bulldozed in 1969 in the redevelopment of New Swindon.

In 1881, The Bull at Highworth was closed and the licence transferred to another new Swindon pub, The Clifton Hotel in Clifton Street which had opened as an off-licence two years earlier. The Carpenters Arms at South Marston was bought the same year.

After a pause of a year, acquisitions started again in 1883 with The Saracens Head, Highworth, and The Running Horse in Swindon bought that year. The New Inn at Stratton and The Angel, Purton, were pur-chased in 1884 and the following year three Swindon pubs were added: The Kings Arms, in Wood Street, The Foresters Arms, in Fleet Street, which was demolished in 1955, and The Gardeners Arms in Westcott Place, which suffered the same fate in 1979.

Two more Swindon pubs - The Lamb and Flag, Bridge Street, and The Masons Arms in High Street - were bought in 1886. The Masons, one of Old Town's oldest buildings, was tragically demolished for road widening in 1969.

The rate of acquisitions then began to slow with The Three Tuns, Wroughton, added in 1889, Black Horse, Wanborough in 1891, Freke Arms, Highworth, in 1892, Bakers Arms, Stratton, and the Plough, Highworth in 1896.

In 1893 The Rising Sun at Wroughton, which had been acquired at an unknown date was sold. In 1897 The County Ground Hotel was built with the licence being transferred from an Arkell beerhouse, The Rampant Cat, in Highworth. The same year The Malt Shovel in Highworth was bought at a closing down auction of the Swindon and North Wiltshire Brewery. This was later demolished and the site incorporated into the car park of the adjoining Fox Inn.

The last 19th century acquisition was The Plough at Stratton, now known as The Rat Trap, which was bought in 1899. The 1890s also saw the rebuilding of several houses, notably the Three Tuns at Wroughton and The Running Horse, Swindon.

But the new century brought problems which put the brakes on the rapid expansion of Arkell's tied estate.

Firstly, the supply of freehouses had dried up and secondly, magistrates had become extremely loath to grant new licences because of the strength of the temperance movement.

In fact, Government legislation was in place to force the closure of thousands of pubs throughout the country. As a result, Arkell's rate of acquisition slowed.

The Rat Trap in 1923.

20

The Wheatsheaf (re-named The Sally Pusseys Inn).

But even against this, the firm still bought The Plough at Fairford in 1900, The Axe and Compass in Wanborough in 1904, and three pubs: The Bakers Arms, Badbury, The Wheatsheaf (now known as The Sally Pusseys Inn) near Wootton Bassett and The Old Bear, Cricklade in 1906. The following year The Plough at Badbury was added, the last pub until the end of World War One.

The magistrates closed The Axe and Compass in Wanborough and The Malt Shovel in Highworth in 1907 and The Fox and Hounds in Wootton Bassett in 1919. The lat-ter had been bought at an unknown date.

More pubs were added between the wars. The Jolly Tar at Hannington and The Royal Oak at Lechlade in 1922, The Duke at Hilmarton in 1923, The George in Lambourne and The Masons Arms in Aldbourne in 1924, and The Bell at Purton Stoke in 1926 - the last pub to be bought before World War Two.

However, this period saw the rebuilding of several pubs, notably The Sun at Coate and The White Hart at Stratton, both of which were much extended. The Crossways Club,

21

later to become The Moonrakers, was built in 1931.

After the war the rapid expansion of Swindon and redevelopment of its town centre had an impact on Arkell's tied estate. However, the first acquisitions were outside the town: The Curriers Arms at Wootton Bassett, The Royal Oak at Bishopstone and The Tavern at Kemble were all added in 1951. The Moonrakers in Swindon became the first pub to get the first entirely new licence granted in Swindon since 1905.

Two new pubs went up in Swindon: The Steam Train in Rodbourne in 1959, its licence coming from the closed Foresters Arms, and the new Carpenters Arms in Gorse Hill in 1964. This, after refurbishment, became known as The Swiss Chalet.

After a few years without an acquisition, The Highwayman at Elkstone between Cirencester and Gloucester was bought in 1972, followed by a group of ex-Trust Houses, The Bull at Fairford and The White Hart at Cricklade in 1973.

In 1976 The Victoria at Eastleach was bought from Courage and in 1979 The George in Fairford was bought, closed and added to the adjoining Bull. A new estate pub, The Liden Arms, opened in Swindon in 1980.

The Duke of Edinburgh at Winkfield, near Ascot, was bought in 1983 marking a significant extension in the area covered by the tied estate and a hint of things to come.

Another new pub, The Woodshaw at Wootton Bassett, was built in 1985. This was followed by the purchase of The Bear in Marlborough in 1987 and The Lord Lyon at Stockcross and Thames Head, Kemble, in 1989.

In 1990 The Masons Arms in Aldbourne was sold off as a free house. The following year

The Carpenters Arms, now called The Swiss Chalet.

22

Managing Director James Arkell toasts the new look St James Hotel, Cheltenham.

marked a first for the Brewery: the purchase of a package of eight pubs from Whitbread. These were: The Plough at Stratton, near Cirencester; The India House, Whitesmiths Arms and Sir Colin Campbell in Gloucester; and The Adam and Eve, Exmouth Arms,

Hereford Arms and St James Hotel in Cheltenham.

Finally, in 1992, The Coopers Arms in Newbury and The Red Lion at Chieveley were bought, adding further to the Eastern side of the tied estate.

CHAPTER THREE

A TRUE FAMILY FIRM

The families behind Arkell's success.

THE ARKELL family has brewed beer for four generations, passing the business on from father to son. In that way the founding traditions of the company have been maintained.

But Arkell's success is based not just on one family but many. The backbone of the company has for generations been the families who make up a large proportion of its staff.

Chairman Peter Arkell is as proud of these families as he is of his own. He believes the company's emphasis on families has inspired loyalty within his staff - making it the envy of many employers.

In most firms nowadays, employees who reach 20 years' service are a rarity. Not so at Arkell's. That length of service is normal. Most employees are introduced by relations, so know about the firm before they get a job.

But once they start working for Arkell's, whether it's in the Brewery, offices or pubs, they discover that it is just like being a member of a big family. Fathers work side by side with their sons, brothers with brothers, mothers alongside daughters and sisters with sisters.

On the rare occasion a vacancy does occur - normally because someone is retiring - one of the staff usually has a relative ready to fill the role. It is rare for Arkell's to advertise.

Peter Arkell believes the way the company treats its staff and their families is the secret of its success. "People spend most of their time at work. If we didn't have a happy atmosphere, they would not stay," he said.

At the frequent barbecues and parties he throws for his staff, their families are invited along too. Arkell's also pays towards the cost of childminders for some staff - a move introduced by the present Chairman Peter Arkell - and provides housing for some.

Arkell's owns houses adjacent to the Brewery. If any staff are interested, all they have to do is put their name down on the waiting list. They don't have to wait long and rents are kept reasonable. "We're not in the property business," he says.

But it's not all honey, Peter admits. People have their good and bad days and just like any other family there are moans and groans.

There's no union – the staff were asked

24

Brewery Directors and staff - Anniversary Year 1993.

but said they didn't want one. But Peter felt there had to be a forum where people aired their problems and could suggest any improvements.

Merv Smith was approached by Peter to set up a Liaison Committee in 1975 with members elected from all sections of the Brewery workforce.

"He was anxious that people who weren't happy could air their views about anything," said Merv. "He was also concerned that, being at the top, he should keep the staff fully informed as to what the directors were plan-

ning and how the Company was doing. It was a great success from the start. He was always there; he never missed!"

Merv joined Arkell's in 1968 after 28 years with the Swindon railworks and ten years as an inspector at car body panel makers Pressed Steel. He was born and raised near the Brewery and had relations who had worked in the bottling plant many years before.

He also knew the Arkell family, having been under-gardener to Captain Graham Arkell, Peter's uncle, at his Beechcroft Road home for a year when he was 14 before he

Brewing in their blood: members of the Dicks, Mercer and Trinder families as well as the Arkell's.

entered the railworks as an apprentice.

"The wage for a boy my age then was around 8-10s a week," remembers Merv. "As under-gardener, I was getting 14s a week, plus a free quarter pint of milk a day, because Capt Arkell had three house cows. I was in seventh heaven!"

Years later when a vacancy came up for a maintenance man to do general repair work on Arkell's pubs, he jumped at the chance. He soon graduated to cellar service, responsible for putting in and maintaining the pumps in all the Arkell's pubs and free-trade.

"I loved the job. Every day would be different," said Merv who retired eight years ago. What struck him most about the Brewery after working in factories was the absence of clocking in - a sign of trust on all sides.

His son Dave, 42, joined the firm in 1970 as a storeman. Merv heard about the vacancy and recommended Dave who was working in the Co-op at the time and wasn't very happy. Merv said: "He was a quiet boy and I knew that Arkell's would suit him better. I wasn't wrong. He's been there 23 years."

Dave added: "I knew I would be happy at Arkell's right from the first day. Everyone was friendly from the start. I knew some of the people because of Dad.

"What I think sums up Arkell's is that every year, everyone gets not only a bonus, but also a chat with the Chairman. He calls the

26

staff up and gives them their bonus plus a little gift and talks to them for a few minutes. The number of hands he has to shake, but he doesn't mind. That sets Arkell's apart from the rest! I couldn't work anywhere else - 23 years service speaks for itself"

The Dicks family are now in their third generation at Arkell's: George, his son Brian, and now Brian's son Chris.

George started at the Brewery washing casks from 1956 before moving on to the fermenting room. He enjoyed his work so much, he carried on part-time until he retired in 1980.

He had been a miner in Derbyshire from the age of 14 but ill-health forced him out and the family moved back to Wiltshire where his wife originally came from.

He worked at the Vickers factory for a short spell until he joined Arkell's.

Brian, his son, now Brewery foreman, remembers him bringing home his beer allowance daily in a jug with a cork top. These jugs were supplied to all Arkell's staff until 1980, when the beer allowance was given weekly in bottles and cans.

"I remember Dad taking it away empty and bringing it back full," said Brian. "Dad loved his beer and was very fond of that jug," said Brian.

Years later, when his father retired, Brian would carry on the tradition at Christmas - bringing home the Christmas brew in his jug.

"He kept telling me I ought to work there and that he would put a word in for me," Brian recalls.

When Brian left school though, it wasn't for Arkell's, but for the building trade. Several other jobs followed including one repairing shoes. George would constantly tell his son that he would be better off at Arkell's, particularly when Brian's son, Chris was born.

In 1964 his dad got his way and Brian joined Arkell's as a driver.

"I think my Dad was more chuffed than me!" he said. But the lure of the building trade proved too strong and he left after three years only to return two years later to work in the mash tun; a job his father had done.

"The Brewery's a part of me"

He learnt all aspects of brewing from the then Head Brewer, Don Kenchington.

In 1990, he became brewhouse foreman replacing Lou Mercer, who retired. Now he couldn't imagine leaving Arkell's a second time.

"The Brewery is a part of me. It would be like cutting off my right arm. That's what my dad used to say and I never completely understood it when I was younger. I certainly do now," said Brian who lives in a Brewery-owned house next door to an Arkell's pub, The Baker's Arms, Statton.

He is in charge of his son Chris, 28, who in contrast started at Arkell's straight from school in 1984 as a cask washer. It was something he always wanted to do.

Although there was plenty of employment around at the time, a job at Arkell's was his one and only ambition.

He'd had holiday jobs at the Brewery before, so knew of the work and the atmosphere. The job he got was in the caskwashing department.

"I had known Arkell's right from the beginning and had even gone in with my Dad when he worked weekends," said Chris. "I knew it was for me. If you did the job, they saw you right. They had always treated Dad well and that's what I wanted. It's important to have a happy and secure atmosphere at work.

"Too good to be true"

"My friends envy me that and the fact that I work with beer – I've got it made haven't I?"

Chris lived in a Brewery-owned cottage in nearby Hyde Rd with a modest rent until two years ago.

Even the cleaning at Arkell's is a family affair. Chris's wife Beverley had also worked at Arkell's as a cleaner with her mum Daphne Binfield.

Sisters Daphne, Maisie Andrews and Annie Perrie were cleaners for Arkell's for over twenty years until 1992. The cleaning is now done by Daphne's daughters.

The Mercer family had three generations working at the Brewery at the same time until 1990 - Lou and his sons Phil and Bob.

Lou retired in 1990 after 30 years in the Brewery, first as bottling manager, then as second brewer. He is delighted and proud his sons work there.

He had been working in the bottling plant of a brewery in Sussex for a only few months when the job at Arkell's came up.

A sales rep he knew from his previous job in Marlborough thought Lou would be ideal for the job but they had lost touch. It took two weeks of long hard searching before he traced Lou and told him to apply.

Lou was very keen as his wife was due to have their first baby. "A company house was a great bonus to go with a good job as we were in lodgings in Horsham. Rooms were hard to find, never mind houses in those days," said Lou.

"I didn't think I would get the job – it seemed too good to be true. Arkell's jobs were snapped up then as they are now because of the good pay and work conditions."

The baby was Phil - now the Brewery's cellar service manager responsible for the quality and condition of the beer and ensuring it keeps in tip-top condition wherever it goes.

But working at Arkell's wasn't his first ambition. It was to join the police force but a twist of fate brought him to Arkell's.

His earliest memory of the Brewery was being taught how to ride a bike in the yard on Christmas Day when he was six by the then-Head Brewer Don Kenchington. "Nobody seemed to mind us kids playing in the yard – it was that sort of place," he said.

Phil grew up in a company house next to the Brewery and used to play with Dave Paginton, son of Tony, who was then bottling foreman. His first job was washing casks, something everybody had to learn. He then went on to cellar service, picking up experience as he went and was made cellar service manager in 1991, when John Hedges retired.

28

A family affair... Lou Mercer (centre) with sons Robert (left) and Philip (right).

He now travels around all Arkell's pubs and anywhere Arkell's has a bar, such as trade fairs and shows.

"This is more than a 9 to 5 job. The condition of the beer doesn't only need to be checked in normal working hours," said Phil. He loves his job and the security and freedom that working for a family firm brings.

"Dad's so happy I work here. He had always wanted me to, because they had been so good to him," added Phil.

His brother Bob, 28, remembers the Brewery as a large, but friendly place, when he was growing up. Phil and Bob used to go in with their father at weekends when he had to work and it always seemed like a big adventure.

"It was so magical seeing all the equipment," said Bob. "It hasn't lost its magic for me today." He used to help out in the summer doing odd jobs and when he left school at 16 there was no question of where he would work.

Bob, too, started in cask washing, replacing Wally Thompson, who had worked at the Brewery for 25 years. He moved on to the Mash Tun in 1983, two years later, replacing Les Rawlings, who was also retiring.

He wouldn't dream of working anywhere else, he says. "They treat you right and nobody is favoured over anyone else." He would like to see his daughter Suzanne, two-and-a-half, and recently-born son Jack working at the brewery. "You couldn't do any better," he said.

Ernie Lane agrees. As the Brewery's longest serving male member of staff with 39 years' service, he speaks from experience. He originally started work in the Brewery's fermenting room, became transport manager but returned to fermenting because that was what he liked doing best.

Ernie, too, had family in the firm. His grandfather Bill was a drayman in the early 1920s when horses and carts delivered the beer and his Uncle Bill was a driver for the Ace Minerals - Arkell's mineral plant which closed in 1962.

Ernie always remembers his family saying his grandfather spoke about Arkell's with fondness and gratitude.

"He always spoke about what good employers they were," said Ernie – and his first wage packet at Arkell's of £3 10s, a good wage at the time, proved it. He knew he was going to stay.

The Head Brewer at the time was 'Smokey' Parsons, who had come out of

Ernie Lane ha at work.

The Arkell's tug-of-war team, early 1930's with Ernie's grandfather Bill (front row 1st from left and father Bill 2nd row 2nd from left).

retirement for six months while Arkell's searched for a suitable replacement for Mr Kirkpatrick, who had died.

"We all called him Smokey because he was never without a pipe in his mouth or a funny story to tell!" said Ernie. "It was a happy atmosphere in the fermenting room. What I couldn't get over was the atmosphere of trust; there was no clocking in or out and there still isn't to this day. You're trusted to do your job and you soon get found out if you don't!".

A year later, Ernie became a drayman and at 19 was promoted to Head Driver in 1972. He then worked in the office working as assistant transport manager. But it didn't suit Ernie and he returned to the fermenting room in 1974 replacing Norman Ward who was retiring after 39 years.

Ernie has lived in various Brewery houses throughout his time at Arkell's, moving to bigger ones as his family increased. He has four children.

"The most important thing to remember is that Arkell's hasn't changed," said Ernie, who joined when Peter Arkell's uncle Graham was in charge.

When Peter joined a new informality came in, said Ernie, although it showed the same loyalties to its staff that it had always done.

"He introduced a more relaxed atmosphere to the company," said Ernie. "When we first met him, he said 'call me Peter,' but nobody could. To call your boss by his first name was too informal, so we decided to call him Mr. Peter and that stuck. He didn't order us to - it just caught on. When Mr. James joined the company, the same thing happened.

"I've seen two Chairmen head this company. Both have made slight changes, but the caring attitude has always been the same."

Margaret Leech, the Brewery's Tied Trade director, became its first female exec-

Tied Trade Director Margaret Leech (left) and her mother Lil.

utive director in 1992. No-one was more pleased than her mum Lil, who has worked at the Brewery for 13 years as its tea lady.

Margaret was already working for Arkell's when Lil heard of the job through a friend.

"Margaret didn't want it to look like favouritism," said Lil. "But when I told her I was interested she was pleased for me and enquired."

Although she knew what Arkell's was like, the atmosphere still surprised her. "They are

31

such nice people. There is no formality. Everyone is treated the same."

Lil also gets a drinks allowance just like everybody else. "There are no favourites. That's what I like best about the firm."

"not a cog in a wheel"

Lil used to do the tea in the mornings and afternoons up until three years ago. The morning shift is now done by Ena Warren, a friend of a friend. There are no drinks vending machines at Arkell's. "Mr Peter likes to have his tea served by people - not machines," laughed Lil.

She is very proud of Margaret's rise through the ranks from an office clerk to Tied Trade Director and believes only a company like Arkell's could have given her the chance.

Margaret joined the Brewery in 1973 as a clerk becoming personal assistant to Managing Director James Arkell five years later. There is another family link - her Uncle Jimmy Williams once worked at the brewery as an engineer.

Sisters Carol and Christine work side by side in stock control and "heave casks with the best of them," they say.

Carol, 58, has been with the company for 43 years since 1950 with a six-and-a-half year break to have her two sons.

She joined the company's bottling store at the age of 15 and remembers her first wage packet of 27s 6d - a fortune for a girl with no qualifications.

She had always wanted to work at the brewery. Her sister, Betty, was already working there and told her of the happy atmosphere.

"The radio was always on and we were never discouraged from singing along. It was always a happy place," said Carol. "You were never just a cog in a wheel, but important. That was and is Arkell's secret - they make you feel important"

Christine joined in 1959, and has served 34 years, 24 of them in the bottling plant. She, too, joined straight from school at the age of 15.

"They encouraged families to work together." she said.

When the bottling plant closed she got a job on stock control. She would never leave Arkell's. "They would have to carry me out! In all the 34 years I have worked there, they have cared about me."

Their nephew Kevin Gleed, 32, drives a fork-lift truck at the Brewery. He joined the bottling store, where his mum Betty Gleed, used to work, in 1978 as a storeman.

He learnt everything from working on the bottle washer to labelling and from mixing lemonades to kegging beer. When the bottling plant closed, Kevin became a drayman before moving onto his present job.

"I've got the best job in the world - a steady wage and security with a company that treats its employees as one big happy family," he said.

Dave Paginton, 36, or Dave the Dray as he is known, also started in the bottling plant, where his father was manager, nearly 19 years ago. His work in those days involved chilling

32

Double act : Tony Paginton and son Dave
outside the former bottling store.

in my own time. Mr. Peter sent me a cheque
for £100 with a note thanking me for my help.
How many people would do that? I still have
that letter to this day."

Trevor Porter is foreman of Arkell's decorating team. He has worked for the company
for 33 years and is due to retire next year. He
loves his job and wouldn't go anywhere else.

"They treat the whole team right. We are
given the same benefits as all the other staff
at Arkell's such as a company pension, drinks
allowance and the chance to rent an Arkell's
house if we want one.

The Arkell's decorating team (bottom to top) :
Graham Compton, Nat Eastman, Trevor Porter
and Phil Thirlaway.

the beer, storing it and racking it ready for
bottling.

Three years later he moved to the transport section and now drives Arkell's beer all
over the country to airshows, functions and to
Arkell's pubs.

His dad Tony had been an engineer but
was out of work when he joined Arkell's in
1967. "It was like a dream come true," he said.

He has many happy memories but one in-
cident sticks in his mind. "It was the year
before bottling closed. We had had some new
machinery installed from abroad, but it
couldn't bottle litres or half litres - only pints
and halves. This posed some problems, because everyone wanted the new-sized bottles.
"I spent months converting the machine

"We also get invited to all the Brewery parties and barbecues. They shouldn't be paying me – I should be paying them!" said Trevor.

Lionel is Trevor's son and originally joined the Brewery in 1966 as a decorator, working alongside his father.

He had always wanted to work at the Brewery, so a couple of years later, he became a drayman, then a cellarman.

In 1988, he left the Brewery for a job with Honda, but missed the Brewery so much he returned to Arkell's cellar three years later.

It was fate that brought him back to Arkell's. A vacancy came up quite by chance.

"I missed the friendly atmosphere that only came with Arkell's and couldn't wait to get back! I didn't know what I had until I lost it. I'm glad I'm back!"

The families that form the backbone of Arkell's don't only work in the Brewery - they also run the pubs.

Families like the Smarts (see panel), Elliotts and Aubreys have brought to life John Arkell's founding tradition of good landlords being as important as good beer.

John Smart (standing far right) by his dray at Cirencester Carnival in 1937 - the year his dray won the "best-dressed" prize.
••••••••••••••••••••••••••••••••••
John Smart has worked for Arkell's for more than 50 years - first as a drayman and then behind the bar. He left his job as a driver for a building firm to become a drayman at the Brewery.

Within a couple of years he was head driver.

"Right from the start, I loved the work," said John, 82. "Although it was heavier because I had to load and unload the lorries I loved the kind working atmosphere and filling my jar with my drinks allowance which I drank after work, of course, because of the driving."

He had always dreamed of running his own pub. His chance came when he met his second wife, Gladys Wiltshire. She ran The Plough in Devizes Road, in Swindon's Old Town, and when they married they ran it together.

"I enjoyed it from the first," said John. "My wife who had run it for 25 years was always helpful. The locals were delighted at the drayman and the landlady getting married and welcomed me with open arms."

When Gladys died in 1983, John's son Roger took over the licence. John still lives above the pub and helps out in the cellar and behind the bar on Sunday lunchtimes.

Roger needed no introduction to the regulars. He wasn't only the landlord's son - he was also a local soccer hero.

He had started out working in the railworks and playing football for Swindon boys and then Wiltshire. But in 1960 at the age of 17 he signed on apprentice terms for Swindon Town.

Roger played 500 matches for Swindon Town in his 13 years with the club - the most memorable being the club's giant-killing 3-1 League Cup victory over Arsenal at Wembley when Roger scored. He later

The Highwayman Inn at Elkstone, near Cheltenham, has also been kept in the family. Landlady Karen Clark's parents ran the nine-room 16th century inn for ten years after Arkell's took it over in 1971.

She followed her parents Vince and Pam Elliott into the trade and, with her husband Jim, managed The Sun Inn at Coate, Swindon, for seven years. But The Highwayman is a special place for Karen. "I have many happy memories and it's such a beautiful place," she said.

Vince and Pam also ran The Sally Pussey's

Family ties: left to right Vince Elliott, Karen and Jim Clark, Pam Elliott at The Highwayman.

Inn near Wootton Bassett and their son Mark also ran The White Hart, at Stratton, Swindon.

The family tie on one Arkell's pub resulted in beer being served at 5p a pint on one special night. The Black Horse at Upper Wanborough, near Swindon, was the first Arkell's pub to win the Campaign for Real Ale regional Pub of the Year.

When licensee Gerry Aubrey was presented with the special certificate in July, he immediately knocked the price of Arkell's 2B bitter down from £1.32 to just 5p a pint for the evening in honour of his father Stan, who ran the pub before him.

Stan ran the pub for 21 years before Gerry took over 15 years ago. Gerry decided to take the price of a pint 36 years ago - roughly two shillings or 10p - and halve it.

played for Charlton and Bath City for four years before hanging up his boots at Trowbridge in 1984.

He never thought about running a pub until his step-mother's death and James Arkell offered him the licence. "It had been my Dad's life and I knew it would break his heart to leave, so I said Yes. He got on so well with Arkell's and they had been so good to him.

"Swindon Town was like a family and so was Arkell's - my Dad said it would be!"

● ● ● ● ● ● ● ● ● ● ● ● ● ● ● ● ● ● ●
Then and now: Roger in his playing days and behind the bar at the Plough.

Success on a plate left to right Alma Nippress, Lynne and Emma Langley at the King's Arms Hotel.

His father would have been proud. The pub and the condition of its beer had beaten hundreds of others across seven counties from Buckinghamshire to the Isle of Wight to win the award.

The Black Horse was nominated by the Swindon CAMRA Branch for its beer, hospitality and general atmosphere as well as the friendliness of its host.

Waitress Lynne Langley started work at the King's Arms in Old Town, Swindon, at the age of 15. Originally a washer-up, after a few years she became a waitress, following in her mother Alma Nippress's footsteps.

Lynne's 17-year-old daughter Emma, also works at the King's Arms part-time, making it three generations of the same family.

To mark Lynne's silver anniversary at the hotel, Peter Arkell presented her with an engraved watch.

Anyone wanting proof that Arkell's is a true family firm need look no further than the company Christmas card. For the past eight years it has been painted by Anne Arkell, wife of Peter.

Slade School-trained Anne has also illustrated beermats, trays and pub signs - the sign for The Highwayman was based on a quick sketch of Peter striking a 'stand and deliver' pose at breakfast one morning.

It seems only right that thousands of Arkell's drinkers rest their glasses on beer-

Anne and Peter at home in front of a mural painted by Anne.

mats showing the Kingsdown Brewery in all its splendour painted by the wife of the Chairman.

Anne and Peter's son James, 42, is now the firm's managing director. He joined the company in 1973 and became a director a year later.

Initially, James was put in the care of his father and Major Bill Eatwell, the brewery's

36

ied trade director at the time.

"Father and the Major taught me virtu-lly all I know," said James. "Father would :all me into meetings or discussions and in he beginning, it wouldn't make much ense, but gradually I began to understand 1bout the business and their love of it)ecame mine, too.

"My father built the company up. His naintenance programme on the houses)ver 20 years ago and the building of new •ubs has paid dividends because the costs vould be so much higher now.

"Although we still spend three-quarters)f a million a year keeping the pubs main-ained and altered, Dad's decisions have :ertainly paid off."

James' admiration of his father is plain to .ee and the success of their relationship is, in)art, responsible for the company's success, ae believes.

"It's true - we gel and that is vital for any ompany to succeed and that's why Arkell's is aot only in business, but succeeding.

"Fathers and sons working together don't .lways get on. The fact that we do makes all he difference. My father and grandfather, >ir Noël, had the same relationship and hat's what I hope to have with my own chil-lren," he says.

James would welcome any of his children: :mma, 17; George, 14; John, 10; and eight-·ear-old Alexander into the business, but the lecision will be theirs, he said. "They've also ;ot to be able to do the job! My own father lidn't force me, but didn't put me off either tnd that's what I will do. It's up to them."

Peter Arkell with his Directors in anniversary Year
FRONT ROW: left to right Margaret Leech, Teresa Hill
BACK ROW:Don Bracher, Nicholas Arkell,
James Arkell, Ray Fisher and Richard Turner.

It was James who made the important decision to buy the package of eight Gloucestershire pubs for around £1.5 million in 1991 - the biggest one-off acquisition in the Brewery's history. It was an important deci-sion to make, but James was backed by his father all the way.

James is also a Lieutenant-Colonel with the Territorial Army, commanding the Royal Yeomanry Regiment of 400 men. He is one of only 14 nationally in the Royal Armoured Corps to hold the position.

Peter Arkell said:"Arkell's is a true fam-ily firm. I don't mind admitting that families are given preference at the Brewery for jobs. That's the way it has been for 150 years and the reason for the company's success. After all, blood is thicker than water!"

37

CHAPTER FOUR

THE ART OF BREWING

A glimpse into the timeless world of brewing at Arkell's.

BREWING beer is a craft almost as old as time itself.

Beer is as much a part of British tradition as the Sunday roast.

Yet brewing is also an art - and despite the onset of technology to almost every aspect of our lives brewing beer is carried out in exactly the same way as it has been for hundreds of years.

In fact, at Arkell's the latest technology has been harnessed not to make any improvements in the way the beer is brewed (how can you improve on perfection anyway)? but to ensure that the beer is top quality every time.

Like most things that bring pleasure, the basic brewing process is relatively simple. And the ingredients that go into Arkell's beer are few. Yet the combination of the very best ingredients and the time-honoured method of brewing employed at Arkell's produces a range of beers renowned wherever real ale is appreciated.

The essential raw material for beer is malted barley. Beer can be brewed using other cereals as base materials including wheat but malt is the tried and tested method of producing real ale.

Barley for brewing is harvested in the normal way but then taken to maltings where it is soaked in water and left so that the germination process can begin.

Head Brewer Don Bracher, left and Robert Mercer check the malt.

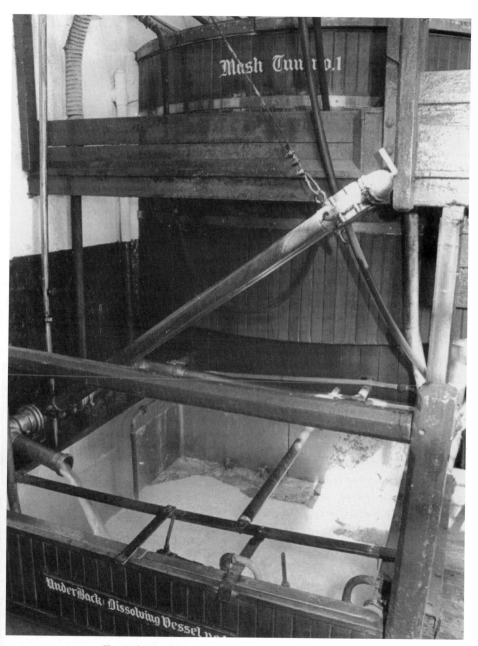

The Mash Tun. The wort can be seen running off (bottom left).

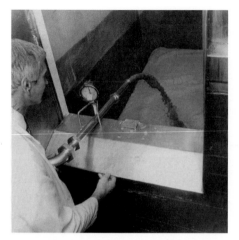

Wort can be seen being pumped into the fermenter.

The malt is then dried in a kiln. Germination stops; it begins to change in colour and the tough barley grain which was full of insoluble starch is now an easily-crushed malt.

It is the different lengths of time malt is heated - and the varying depths of brown it goes - that gives us different types of real ale.

Light brown malt is ideal for pale ales but when it is roasted for longer it goes darker and becomes the basic ingredient for darker beers.

Arkell's adds different proportions of darker or 'crystal' malt to its range of beers to give each its own distinctive flavour and colour. For instance, the crystal malt in 3B not only gives a fullness to the malty flavour but also its amber colour. By adding black or 'chocolate' malt to Mash Tun Mild, the beer has a darker colour and roasted malty taste.

Arkell's malts come mainly from East Anglia. When they arrive at the Kingsdown

Brewery the different malts are selected and lightly crushed in a mill to form a coarse flour known as grist. It is now ready to play its part in the first stage of the brewing process.

The grist is mixed in a device called a steels masher with hot water or, as water is always known in the brewing process, liquor. Arkell's uses water from the local supply but treats it by adding essential mineral salts for flavour and to help the yeast grow.

The porridge-like mixture, now called goods, is run in to the mash tun, a huge container, and left for up to two hours. The process is a little like brewing tea - hence the phrase mashing - but mention this to a brewer and you will get short shrift. With beer the temperature and time are very precise and

The second day of fermentation; the rocky head will soon become a creamy one.

critical to the final product - nothing like brewing a cuppa!

The strong, sugary mixture which emerges from this process is called wort. It is drained through the slatted bottom of the mash tun and pumped to the copper. Hot liquor is sprayed over the mash - this process is known as sparging - to ensure all the sugar solution gets through to the copper.

The grains left behind in the mash tun, although still high in protein, are now no good for brewing. They are sold as animal feed.

Now it is time to add the hops. These not only add bitterness to the beer but also act as a natural preservative.

The characteristic flavours of real ales

Don Bracher checks the boil after the hops have been added.

come from the resins and oils in the tiny glands in the hop cones. These dissolve when they are boiled with the wort in the copper. Like malt, different varieties of hops produce different flavours and aromas in beer. There is a wide selection of hops available to brewers. Arkell's uses only traditional British varieties of Fuggles and Goldings from the hop fields of Hereford, Worcester and Kent.

The wort and hops are boiled together for just over an hour - a process which also sterilises the wort. The mixture, now called hopped wort, is run out the bottom of the copper into a hop back where the spent hops are drained off. These are used for fertiliser.

The hopped wort has to be cooled to around 17 degrees C and oxygenated before it is ready for the next ingredient that also adds its own character and flavour to Arkell's quality beers: yeast. It is yeast that turns the natural sugar in the hopped wort into alcohol – a process known as fermentation.

But at Arkell's it is not just any old yeast.

41

Brewing foreman Brian Dicks (left) and Don Bracher check the gravity of the beer before racking into casks.

The same family of yeast is being used as in the 1930s. The near-magic properties of yeast means that it never runs out. However, just in case, Arkell's keeps a strain of its unique yeast in a national yeast bank.

Family brewers like Arkell's nurture and protect their yeast because of its vital role in giving their beer its own unique flavour. Because it multiplies by about four times its original size during the brewing process it never runs out. In fact there is always a surplus after each brew. Some is kept under refrigeration to start the process again and some is sold for food products, particularly health foods because it is rich in vitamin B complex.

The gravity or density of the sugar solution is important for the strength and final alcoholic content of each beer. The original gravity of Arkell's beers are: 2B:1032, 3B:1040 and Kingsdown:1052.

It is part of the brewer's art to control the amount of fermentation to obtain the right balance between alcohol content and the desired flavour. He is able to do this by cooling the beer in the fermenter and preventing excessive heat which could also damage the yeast and spoil the beer.

42

Casks being filled. This process is known as racking.

The beer is fermented for up to five days; the yeast initially producing a large, rocky head which gradually changes to a creamy, smooth head. Carbon Dioxide is also given off by the yeast.

Although there are no more ingredients to add the beer is still not ready; at this stage it is called "green" beer.It now has to rest and mature. It does this in metal casks - hence the term cask-conditioned.

Finings are added to clarify the beer but some traces of yeast still in the beer produce carbon dioxide, giving it a sparkle and flavour.Stronger beers need longer to mature but even Arkell's lowest gravity beer 2B takes 14 days to produce from the mash.

Only then is it ready to satisfy the discerning Arkell's drinker.

43

CHAPTER FIVE

"THE BEST JOB IN THE WORLD"

Three Arkell's Head Brewers tell their stories.

THE SUCCESS of any brewery depends, first and foremost, on its beer and that means on its Head Brewer.

It is the skill and dedication of this man that ensures each pint is as good as it can be. Quality is all important in brewing; from the raw materials to the finished product.

The priority for this man in the white coat is to make sure Arkell's beers always taste excellent. But there is much more to it than there seems.

Over the last 38 years the head brewer's chair at Arkell's has been occupied by just three men; each with their own views on brewing and stories to tell.

R. HOLGATE-SMITH (1955-1967)

Mr Holgate Smith is now 92. Although he is hard of hearing and his eyesight is failing, his memories of his time at the Brewery are crystal clear.

"I came into brewing after the First World War and needed a job," he recalled."My father and grandfather were brewers and so it ran in the family. My father was concerned about me going into brewing because at that time, takeover bids had already started and small, family concerns were being swallowed up.

"There was a lot of uncertainty around then after the war and not a lot of good, steady jobs around. I trained on the job, so to speak. There were none of the fancy courses then that there are now. I learnt by experience. I soon realised the magic that brewing holds for anyone that falls under its spell."

The industry that Mr Holgate-Smith entered as a teenager was a far cry from what it is today, with many more small family-owned breweries and the days of the nationally-sold brands of beer a generation away.

But the job of brewer was then, as it is now, about challenges.

"The challenge that malt and hops present

when they are left over from one year to the next. How to make last year's taste as good as this year's. That was the challenge and that is also the secret of good beer: consistency."

Mr Holgate-Smith honed this secret to perfection and brought it with him to Arkell's. The company's previous long-serving Head Brewer, David Kirkpatrick, had died in his chair and a retired brewer, Mr Parsons, had been holding the fort for six months until the company found the right man for the job.

Arkell's found him in Mr Holgate-Smith. He came to Wiltshire from a brewery in Scotland. It was a much larger concern and he was interested in moving back South and to a family brewer. And, like many before and after him, he fell in love with Arkell's the minute he walked through the Brewery gates.

"It was like coming home," he recalled, "Mr Graham and Mr Noël were gentlemen - there's no other way to describe them.

"And when they got my references from my previous employer, instead of just writing to let me know I'd got the job, Mr Graham said:'We are both lucky.' That's when I knew that I was going to be happy there."

And happy he was. Mick, as he was called by a select few although no one knew what the R in his name stood for, spent over 15 years at the Brewery as Head Brewer. Responsibility at the time was not only for the Brewery, but the mineral and bottling plants which were both then on the site.

"Brewing was more than a full-time job

then. We brewed four days a week, but fermenting was a seven day job and so I always had to be on hand," said Mr Holgate-Smith, who had a reputation as a perfectionist.

His hours were meant to be 8am until about 6pm, but as he lived on the premises in a rent-free Brewery house, he was around far longer than that - sometimes till about 10pm, checking everything.

"I loved it there. It was my life"

"I loved it there. It was my life and I used to enjoy walking round, checking everything was OK."

Mr Holgate-Smith retired in 1967 at the age of 66. His decision to leave was prompted by the conversion of the Brewery from coal-fired heating to oil-fired.

"I decided that all the upheaval was not for me and to make way for a younger man," he said.

The man appointed was Don Kenchington, who was then Arkell's Second Brewer and Bottling Manager.

"Don was perfect for the job," said Mr Holgate-Smith. "Even though he had little experience of brewing when he first came, I knew he would be right, because of his naval experience. Loyalty, discipline and cleanliness - it was all in the naval training. Right from the time he was Second Brewer, he had his training on the job - the best training you can get!"

Mr Holgate-Smith went to live in a cottage in the picturesque village of Biddestone near Chippenham but due to ill health returned to Swindon, where he now lives.

DON KENCHINGTON 1967-1991

When Don Kenchington retired as Head Brewer, it was estimated he had brewed around one-and-a-half billion pints for Arkell's. And he enjoyed making every single one of them.

A warm, larger-than-life character with a lively sense of humour, Don holds the record as the longest-serving Arkell's Head Brewer. To the fact that he has brewed all those pints he adds, jokily, "I've lost count of how many I've drunk!"

He lives by the Brewery in a company house. It was ordered to be built specially for him by Chairman Peter Arkell.

Don had been Bottling Manager for ten years and Second Brewer for eight when appointed Mr Holgate-Smith's successor.

The change in character could not have been more stark. With his infectious laugh and out-going nature against Mr Holgate-Smith's traditional outlook, Don brought a new informality to the Brewery. His staff called him Mr K. or "Ken" — something unheard of under Mr Holgate-Smith.

But it was not a foregone conclusion Don would get the job.

"I had a feeling I would be Head Brewer because two years earlier, a head brewer's job had come up in Cornwall. Mr.Holgate-Smith asked me why I hadn't gone for the job. I replied that I was happy at Arkell's and would be happy to stay as Second Brewer for the rest of my life. And that was the truth! I was *really* happy!"

46

Unlike his predecessor, who had always been a brewer, Don had spent the majority of his working life in bottling as well as a spell in the Navy before joining Arkell's. His first job at 16 was bottle washing in a brewery. After that he progressed up the ladder in bottling departments at breweries in Birmingham and Chichester, his home town.

He first learnt about the Bottling Manager's job at Arkell's from Norman Cornwall, a rep who was visiting the brewery where he was then working.

"He told me the place would be ideal for me. I was getting fed up with the job I was doing at the time and wanted to move on," said Don.

"You had to wait to fill a dead man's shoes there and I was ready to move on. Norman put a word in for me and I saw Mr Graham and Sir Noël, who were joint MD's at the time and Mr Holgate-Smith. I was offered the job shortly after that.

"I remember thinking as I looked round that I would be happy and I wouldn't want to move on. Arkell's was and is a happy place. The recommendation from Norman changed my life and I will always be grateful to him for that.

"I also had three young daughters under five and wanted to stay put somewhere because of their schooling. This move had to be the right one."

As Head Brewer, Don knew the ropes. His eight-year stint as Second Brewer under Mr Holgate-Smith had taught him everything he needed to know.

"I learnt a lot from Mr. Holgate-Smith,"

said Don. "I had been involved a little bit with brewing before my time at Arkell's, but Mr Holgate-Smith's experience was invaluable to me and taught me a lot. I also went on courses, but nothing beats hands-on experience."

Don in turn taught Lou Mercer, who became his Second Brewer.

Don's expertise reaped rewards. He won second prize for 3B in a national competition run by the Sunday Express in 1983. Every regional brewer in the country had entered. He also won top prize in the Sunday Express for his Royal Wedding Ale which commemorated the 1981 wedding of the Prince and Princess of Wales.

As well as brewing beer he also had another very important job - inspecting the new toilets in Arkell's refurbished pubs!

When Peter Arkell joined the company in

"...nothing beats hands - on experience."

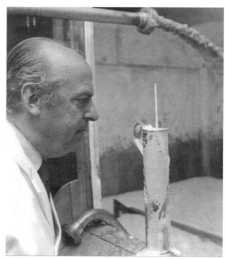

47

Don Kenchington celebrates retirement with his 1.5 billionth pint.

1956, his reponsibilities included the tied houses. He started a massive refurbishment programme.

"The big thing with him was the toilets. He used to say if the ladies' toilet wasn't right we would never get the wives and girlfriends in!" remembered Don. "He would always ask me to inspect them and give me his opinion. I remember one of the first was The George at Kempsford. He asked me to give it the once over and I remember thinking it was so nice the Queen could take a pee in it!" Don laughed!

Don struck up a very special relationship with Peter.

"We were around the same age and had joined the company at the same time. I admired him and the things he was doing, particularly with pub catering. A lot of pubs just offered crisps and a pickled egg for a bar meal then. Peter saw that as the way ahead and did it. Our pubs were the envy of many. As well as good beer, you had to have good food."

Don was made a director in 1970; a move that surprised and delighted him.

"In those days it was unusual for a private family brewery to make employees directors. Peter and Arkell's were first with that, too," said Don.

When Don decided to retire his job didn'

48

ARKELL'S BOTTLED BEERS DOWN THE YEARS.
HOW MANY DO YOU RECOGNISE?

Arkell's stout was first launched in the 1950s, several designs for the brand came and went. This one's from 1966.

A firm favourite with Arkell's drinkers since the early 1930s, this is from the late 1950s.

The first 2B label from 1937 when it was known as Pale Ale. This is also the year Arkell's bottling plant opened.

This label is from 1978. Arkell Shandy, abv 2%, was a big hit with children, teenagers and their parents!

Brown Ale was first launched by Arkell's in the 1930s. This is a label from 1974, four decades later.

This is a 2B label from 1972 when it was known as Pale Ale. Bottled 2B underwent several names until, in the late 1970s, it became 2B by popular demand.

As one of Arkell's oldest brands, it's hardly surprising that 3B has undergone several label design changes. This is from 1969.

This was launched in 1969 following the huge success of the limited edition Cup Final Ale. It was simply Cup Final Ale with a new name.

Arkell's changed the name of its Brown Ale to Brown Jack in 1976 - in honour of a local 1930s racehorse which won the Ascot Gold Cup.

The latest 3B bottled design in colours reminiscent of the GWR. Railworkers were among John Arkell's first customers in 1843.

Another design change for 3B, Arkell's flagship brand. Here's one from 1976.

Although launched in bottled form in 1977, the label has been changed several times. Here is a 1978 design.

COMMEMORATIVE ALES

Produced in 1981 to celebrate the wedding of Charles and Diana, this beer was voted best Royal Wedding Ale in a national competition.

Brewed to celebrate Swindon Town FC's Wembley appearance in the 1969 League Cup final. STFC's nickname is The Robins.

Arkell's were commissioned to brew this commemorative beer, to celebrate Paddington Station's 125th anniversary in 1979.

This ale was produced as a strictly limited edition in 1993, the Brewery's 150th anniversary year. See Chapter Six.

THE ARKELL'S BREW

❶ THE MILL. This is where the malt is crushed.

❷ GRIST CASE. The crushed malt collects here.

❸ MASH TUN. The malt is mixed with water at this stage.

❹ UNDERBACK. (Sugar dissolving vessel). This is where sugar is added to the malt and water mixture.

❺ COPPER. The sugar, malt and water mixture, now known as wort, collects here. Hops are then added to the mixture.

❻ HOPBACK. The spent hops are strained here.

❼ PARAFLOW. This is also known as a heat exchanger or wort cooler because the wort is aerated and cooled here. At this stage fermentation can begin.

❽ ARKELL'S YEAST. The yeast, which helps to give Arkell's beers their distinctive flavour, is kept here.

❾ FERMENTER. This is where yeast is added and fermentation takes place.

❿ CASK RACKING. The beer is transferred to casks here and left a few weeks to mature. Only then is it ready to satisfy the discerning Arkell's drinker.

Anyone wanting proof tha
Arkell's is a true family fir
need look no further than th
company Christmas card. Fo
the past eight years it has bee
painted by Anne Arkell.

Slade School - trained Ann
has also illustrated for beer
mats, tray and pub signs. I
seems only right that thousand
of Arkell's drinkers rest thei
glasses on beermats showin
the Kingsdown Brewery in all it
splendour painted by the wife c
the Chairman. (See page 36)

need to be advertised.

"Word got around and lots of people applied," said Don. He also asked other brewers for their recommendations, including Bill Mellor at Abingdon-based Morland's.

"Straightaway, he recommended his second brewer, Don Bracher. I had met Don at several social occasions, such as bowling at Morland's. Brewers are a very friendly bunch and often have get-togethers. Don's immense knowledge of brewing wasn't the only thing that convinced me he was right. I knew our anniversary year was coming up and there would be lots of demands on the Head Brewer.

"Brewers have to have the right person-ality and Don has. His dedication, professionalism and love of Arkell's and its beers got him the job. I've had the best job in the world and now he has."

Don Kenchington still pops into the Brewery as his house is in the grounds. In fact, he is often behind the bar in the cellar pulling pints for visitors just as he did when he was Head Brewer. The only difference now is someone else has brewed the beer. Arkell's is still a way of life for him.

"When I stand outside my house, I see green land, foxes and all sorts of wildlife. If I hadn't worked at Arkell's I wouldn't have all this," he added.

"I've had the best job in the world and now he has." Don Kenchington (left) hands over to Don Bracher.

DON BRACHER 1992 to the present day.

Don Bracher joined the company as it was about to embark on probably the most hectic 12 months in its history: its 150th anniversary year. All kinds of things were about to happen. But what pleased Don most were reports back from Arkell's drinkers in the pubs that the beer hadn't changed: the biggest compliment a brewer can receive.

"That's the way I like it," said Don, 43. "Arkell's beer should taste like Arkell's beer."

Don likes to be in the thick of it in the brewhouse among all the equipment and chaos associated with the art of brewing. His appointment at Arkell's was the realisation of

a long-cherished dream.

"I had always wanted to work for a sma regional brewer. The company is high respected in the trade and its honourable re utation preceded it. I also wanted to be a bi fish in a small pool rather than the vast ocear I had been in."

These had included a spell with Watne Mann in London where he started as a traine shift brewer and worked his way up, then ont Morland's.

"Watney Mann's estate had over 3,0C pubs, Morland's a couple of hundred ar Arkell's just over 80. So I worked my way dow in barrelage. But I wouldn't have had it ar

54

other way. As Head Brewer at Arkell's I am doing a bit of everything, not just sitting in an office, shuffling pieces of paper around.

"I'm still involved in brewing in a hands-on way - from mashing to fermenting. The job presents all the challenges I wanted - to keep the beers up to the consistent quality they have always been and to create the new Anniversary beer."

Don is the only Arkell's Head Brewer who went back to school. He realised his degree in Zoology from Exeter University was not the most obvious for a brewer. He also did not want to become what he describes as a 'push button' brewer. So he left Watney Mann in 1976 and studied malting and brewing science at Birmingham University leaving with an MSc after his name.

He was not always destined for a career in brewing. When he left Exeter University he nearly joined the RAF. Instead, his liking for beer and his science background led him almost at the last minute to opt for brewing.

Like Mr Holgate-Smith, Don sees challenges in brewing. Having barely got his feet under the desk he was involved in getting Mash Tun Mild down in strength, and price, after requests for change from Arkell's drinkers.

He was responsible for brewing the special RAF Ale to commemorate its 75th anniversary and then, his biggest challenge, to brew a celebratory ale for Arkell's 150th anniversary. He consulted several of Arkell's brewing records and also tapped the enormous knowledge of his predecessor, Don Kenchington, who had produced several anniversary beers.

The result was 3A - Arkell's Anniversary Ale - a strong golden beer and a fitting tribute not only to Don but to all his predecessors at the Brewery.

"It was an honour to create this special beer and also the look that went with it: the black and gold labels and pump clips and the special limited edition boxed four packs," said Don.

Wasps are always a problem in a brewery. They are attracted by the smell of the beer and, in the days before wasp bait, were quite a pest.

This is how the three Head Brewers dealt with them in their day and in Don Bracher's case-the present day.

MR. R. HOLGATE-SMITH

"I was terrified of wasps but they had to be kept at bay. Chemical flykiller sprays couldn't be used as they would have affected the taste of the beer. So I had a secret weapon to keep them at bay - my fingers!

In September every year, wasps would gather round my office window. They were attracted by the smell of the beer. I was terrified of them. I used to flick them off my windowsill. I got 92 in a day once, but never got my century!"

DON KENCHINGTON

"In my time wasp bait was introduced and virtually solved the problem, but the odd one got in. That was when my big fat ruler came in handy. I just squashed them with it!

DON BRACHER

Don's ruler must have done a good job of scaring them off, because I haven't seen any anywhere!

CHAPTER SIX

BEERS DOWN THE YEARS

Arkell's beers, now and then.

ARKELL'S has always been renowned for its fine beers and has remained true to its founding traditions despite the passing of time.

Over the years brown, mild, stout and keg bitter have all been firm favourites only to lose their popularity as tastes and fashions have changed.But beers such as best bitter have a timeless appeal - which is why Arkell's 3B has been brewed continually since the early part of this century.

Beer labels too, have changed over the years, reflecting different fashions and trends.

Some Arkell's brands are now just a fond memory for beer drinkers. Others are still going strong, enjoyed by new generations of discerning drinkers.

Bottled, one-off, limited edition and commemorative beers have been popular, but are brewed less often by Arkell's since the closure of its bottling plant in 1981.

However, that did not stop it producing its excellent 3A, Arkell's Anniversary Ale, in its anniversary year of 1993.

Here is a list of main Arkell's brands past and present. Some you will instantly recognise, others will take a little longer.

Thank you for your kindness,
Best wishes,
David Hempleman-Adams

3B reaches the parts... Explorer David Hempleman-Adams celebrates at the North Pole with a bottle of 3B. Arkell's helped sponsor his trip.

ARKELL'S BEERS OF TODAY

3B

Originally brewed around 1910 and sold nder its full name Best Bitter Beer, 3B soon came a best seller. But the name was a bit 'a mouthful and was soon shortened to BBB d then 3B by customers.

The beer has been Arkell's flagship brand r many years and has been in constant pro-ction. Popularity really grew in the 1970s hen real ales came back into fashion because ' pressure from CAMRA (Campaign for eal Ale). A bottled version was introduced the 1950s.

As the beer is one of the oldest surviving oduced by the Brewery, the bottle label has undergone many design changes. The beer has now been totally repackaged to give it a new look with racing green, gold and red; the colours are reminiscent of the Great Western Rail-way. The Brewery had strong links since its earliest days with the GWR.

It has an original gravity 1040 and an abv (alcohol by vol-ume) 4.0%. It is a notable amber coloured beer, full-bodied with a well balanced malt and hop flavour, leaving a lingering dry finish.

57

With an original gravity of 1033 or abv 3.2%, 2B is a refreshing lower gravity beer with a full, satisfying flavour.

KINGSDOWN ALE

First brewed in 1976 on draught and introduced in bottled form the following year. Canned version introduced in 1978.

Kingsdown is a splendid rich coloured strong beer with a distinct malt and hop flavour. It was originally brewed as a commemorative ale in honour of Swindon Town FC's League Cup final appearance in 1969 (See page 60)

NORTH STAR KEG

Brewery conditioned version of 3B but retaining its flavour and not highly gassed. Also darker and sweeter.

First introduced in late 1970s. Very popular on the club circuits where it is known as Brewery conditioned 3B (BC3B).

Original gravity 1036, abv 3.6% .

MASH TUN MILD

This gives drinkers a taste of nostalgia, as it is based on Home-Brewed,

2B

Also first brewed in the early 1900's and constantly brewed since then. First bottled in 1937. Bottled 2B is very popular mixed with draught 3B - known as light and bitter.

Originally this was the Brewery's most popular brand but was overtaken in the 1970s by 3B.

For a time, in the 1970s, there was a name change to John Arkell Bitter but it reverted back to 2B by popular demand.

Called Pale Ale and then Light Ale in bottled form since the 1930s, changed to 2B in the late 1970s.

Arkell's popular bottled mild. After success-
ful trials on draught in selected Arkell's pubs
it went on more general release in 1991.

Mash Tun's smooth, sweet flavour brings
back the taste of traditional mild and has an
original gravity of 1042, abv 4.2% per cent.

NOËL ALE

Launched in 1987 and named in honour
f Sir Noël Arkell who was born on Christmas
Day. The late Sir Noël is the father of the
Chairman, Peter Arkell.

This beer, with its strong, full-bodied
avour and distinctive light colour, is guar-
nteed to warm the heart of any beer drinker.

With an original gravity of 1055, abv 5.5%;
is the strongest of Arkell's current beers.
Toël Ale is only available in December.

ARKELL'S ANNIVERSARY ALE (3A)

To mark its 150th anniversary present
Head Brewer Don Bracher and his predecessor Don Kenchington got together to brew a
special ale. They came up with Arkell's
Anniversary Ale: a golden, well balanced,
strong beer with a malty and hoppy flavour.

3A was brewed at an original gravity of
1070, abv of over 6%, making it the strongest
Arkell's beer ever to go on draught. The gold-
en colour was chosen to make it distinctive.

The beer was initially available only in
275ml bottles in packs of four in a special
commemorative pack of black and gold, the
company's anniversary colours. Only 2,000
boxes (8,000 bottles) were produced. Arkell's
shareholders and employees received packs
while others were presented at official functions and to winners of the Arkell's
Anniversary Passport Promotion. The bottled
version was slightly stronger with an original
gravity of 1075, abv of over 6%.

3A went on draught for a short period in
September 1993.

59

ARKELL'S BEERS OF YESTERYEAR

KING KEG

Originally launched in the 1960's when keg beer was the "in-drink", this beer enjoyed huge success for many years and was withdrawn when, due to the pressure of CAMRA, real ale started to enjoy a huge revival.

Pale, full-bodied bitter beer with a hoppy after-flavour.King Keg was a combination of Keg 3B and 2B.

Was replaced by North Star Keg.

HOME BREWED

A pasteurized bottled mild ale. This was popular for many years. First launched by Arkell's in 1937, it was a soft, mild ale with a malty taste.

This was dropped in the 1960's due to declining popularity of mild and bitter.

Original gravity of between 1031 and 1032.

ARKELL SHANDY

First launched in 1978. This was very popular with children, teenagers and their parents because its alcohol content was under 2%! Made with Arkell's own lemonade and King Keg and then North Star Keg. Stopped production with the closure of Arkell's bottling plant in the early 1980s.

ARKELL'S CUP FINAL ALE

This ale was produced specially to commemorate Swindon Town FC's Wembley appearance in the League Cup final of 1969 when the club won a famous victory over

Arsenal. It was strictly a limited edition. The label features a robin, after STFC's nickname, the Swindon Robins.

It proved so popular it was relaunched immediately on draught as Strong Ale and then renamed in 1976 Kingsdown Ale, giving it a stronger brewery link.

Original gravity 1050, abv 5%.

ARKELL'S BITTER

This beer was specially produced in 1979 to celebrate the 125th anniversary of Paddington Station.

Arkell's was commissioned to produce this celebratory ale by British Rail, who then sold it on its trains and station bars.

It had an original gravity of 1034, abv 3.4%, and was a light-coloured full flavoured light ale with a nice, hoppy flavour.

GWR ALE

Specially brewed to celebrate the 150th anniversary of the Great Western Railway.

Arkell's was specially commissioned to produce the beer, which was then distributed by BR to selected railway station bars. The beer was a high gravity light ale with a strong barley wine-style flavour.

Original gravity 1042, abv 5%.

ROYAL WEDDING ALE

Specially brewed by Don Kenchington, Arkell's Head Brewer at the time, to celebrate the wedding of Charles and Diana in 1981. It was a sweet, golden ale with a powerful kick at the back of the throat. This beer was voted top Wedding Ale out of fourteen others in a competition run by the Sunday Express.

Chariots of Fire director Colin Welland and actress Gemma Craven were among the judges.

Original gravity 1081, abv 8%.

ARKELL'S STOUT

First launched in bottle in the 1950s, this remained very popular until the 1960s when due to declining popularity, production was stopped.

BROWN JACK BROWN ALE

This was Arkell's ale with a label designed and named after the Ascot Gold Cup winner of the 1930s. Brown Jack remains the best-loved local racehorse in an area which has seen its fair share of champions.

Discontinued in 1981 due to falling popularity and the closure of the bottling plant.

Original gravity 1040, abv 4%.

RAF ANNIVERSARY ALE

Arkell's beat off stiff competition to be awarded the contract to brew the RAF Anniversary Ale – specially produced to celebrate the 75th anniversary of the Royal Air Force.

It was to be a double celebration. The ale with its distinctive can design in RAF colours was brewed in Arkell's 150th anniversary year.

The family firm produced almost 100,000 cans of the brew, which was available throughout the UK, in supermarket chains as well as NAAFI clubs and RAF bases nationwide.

The Ale has a distinctive malt and fruit flavour and is pleasantly warming with an original gravity of 1050 or abv of 5%.

For every can sold, 3p was donated to the RAF Benevolent Fund.

An old Arkell's ad, reflecting the taste of the 1960s
taken from The Evening Advertiser July 30th 1964,
courtesy of Wiltshire Newspapers.

CHAPTER SEVEN

BOTTLING - THE ULTIMATE REFINEMENT

The story of Arkell's bottling plant, 1937 to 1983.

IN the summer of 1937, Arkell's opened its bottling plant. The demand for bottled beers had never been higher. The technology of the 1930s was nothing like it is today, and this meant that the quality of draught beer was variable from pub to pub.

This is why the British public liked to mix their draught beer with bottled. Mild and bitter and light and bitter were both popular at the time.

Tony Paginton, Arkell's Bottling Manager from the early 1960s until it closed in 1983 said: "With a bottle, you knew exactly what you were getting: a decent beer with a bit of bubble."

The major investment in bottling during the 1930s signified a big change for the Brewery. Previously it had only produced draught beers, but a growing taste for drinks such as light and bitter and mild and bitter fuelled demand and spurred the company into action. The take-home market was also growing which made being able to sell bottled beers more important.

Arkell's bottled three of its own beers to start with: Home-Brewed, Pale Ale and Stout. Later it added Guinness, which was common amongst breweries at the time. Huge hogsheads of Guinness would arrive at the brewery for bottling in the same way as home-produced beers, but it obviously brought in much-needed revenue.

Thousands of pounds were spent in setting up the bottling plant in 1937. But the plant was put to good use and by 1938 was reported to be filling 1,440 bottles of beer an hour. The bottles themselves had long life-spans and could be expected to be used about 60 times before being discarded or damaged.

64

Bottling Plant Staff c. 1950s
The Head Brewer at the time, Mr Kirkpatrick is on the far right.

HOW BEER WAS BOTTLED IN 1937

To a pre-War generation, Arkell's bottling plant was definitely considered hi-tech. A highly-detailed article in the Evening Advertiser of 14 May 1938 describes, under the sub-heading of "Marvels of scientific control at Kingsdown Brewery" how the bottles were prepared for filling and how the beer was prepared for them.

The writer, obviously an admirer of Arkell's beers, paints a wonderful picture in the article of the bottling plant at work.

Bottling beer, the article says, "incorporates the ultimate refinement of the brewer's craft." And it continues: "When you call, as several thousand people do daily, for an Arkell's bottled beer; when you pour it, clear and sparkling, into your glass, you do not think perhaps, of all the machinery and hygiene necessary to ensure that it shall be delightful to the taste and to the eye."

The article records how returned bottles are prepared. "The bottle arrives, in company with dozens of others, in a large wooden crate. It is dirty inside, its label is torn and maybe its stopper wants seeing to. The stopper is removed and the bottle is placed in a big automatic washing machine. It fits, neck

65

downwards, into a niche on a moving tray and soon it is in the interior of the machine, being sprayed, inside and out, by a powerful douche of hot water.

"This is only a preliminary rinse. The bottle goes on to a caustic jet which injects it with caustic soda at a temperature of 130 degrees Fahrenheit."After all this automation it is refreshing to read that the human touch had not disappeared.

"A girl removes it and holds it up at once to a bright light, to see that the washing has been thoroughly and efficiently done and that the bottle contains no imperfections. If everything satisfies her it goes on to be dried," the article recounts. The article details the complex process the beer had to go through to prepare it for bottling. The beer was transported across the brewery yard from the fermenting tanks to the bottling plant to be conditioned.

This took between seven and ten days. As well as conditioning "in large gleaming white tanks lined with glass" (instead of in casks like draught beer) the beer needed carbon dioxide added to it.

Cast of TV's popular comedy show "Please Sir" on a visit to the bottling plant in the early 1970s. Bottling Manager Tony Paginton is at the front, far right.

A general view of part of the brewery in 1937, the year the bottling store opened for business. The bottling store is on the left.

"Fermentation alone is not enough to produce the soft sparkle and clear appearance which discriminating people look for in the modern bottled beer," the article explains.

After carbonation the beer went into large tanks in the cold room. "And this room certainly is a cold place," the article says. "To go into it suddenly is like stepping from June sunshine to January frost."

But the human touch - or rather taste - is important here as well.

"There is no mechanical way of testing beer to see if it has just the right taste and is aerated to the right extent," the article continues. "This can only be done by the human tongue and by the judgment and experience of the taster. To sample the beer constantly is the not unenviable job of the head brewer, who can tell at a sip whether the beer is 'just right'."

And the article finishes with this piece of advice for drinkers of bottled beer;"We have watched the whole bottling process. We have seen how the bottles are prepared for the beer and how the beer is prepared for the bottles. We have seen the two meet."

67

"Next time you call for an Arkell's Home Brewed, Pale Ale or bottled Stout, think of its complex, well-cared 'home life'."

THE END OF AN ERA

The bottling plant closed in 1983 due to falling sales of its products.Draught beer had improved tremendously from the 1930s and drinkers no longer needed to mix draught and bottled products to get a decent pint.

The age when mild and bitter was a firm favourite had come to an end. Take-home trade, once dominated by the bottle, had been overtaken by the can revolution. Arkell's had started canning its own beers in 1977, due to public demand, placing a contract with Banks's of Wolverhampton at the time.

Stout was no longer fashionable with women. The arrival of Babycham in the 1960s had seen to that. So Arkell's got rid of the pasteuriser that in its heyday had been set aside one day a week just for stout.

The signs that the bottle market was to be fragmented had started a decade before the closure of Arkell's bottling plant. What dwindling market there was had started to be captured by much larger companies.

Tony Paginton recalls:"Arkell's kept bottling going as long as it could, but cuts had to be made to keep the plant going. As staff left, they were not replaced and in the late 1970s the company even started to make its own bottled lemonade again as well as shandy in an effort to keep the plant productive."

Tony used to enjoy his work in his little hut next to the brewery car park mixing the syrups for the lemonade.The lemonade was

supplied to all Arkell's pubs and offered to the free trade, but once again the big boys - Coca Cola and Britvic - had started to dominate the market by their huge marketing spends.

Competition from the larger soft drinks companies had forced the closure of the mineral plant in 1962. After 29 years in business the company's brand name, Ace had been sold so multi-million slick advertising campaigns fought the soft drinks war - and won.

Tony recalls:"Our cola and lemonade was just as good as the others, but those drinks were what people wanted and we had to start buying them in."

Arkell's wasn't the only brewery hit by falling bottled sales; it happened everywhere.

In its heyday the company had bottled four days a week with another day allocated for cleaning equipment. By the end, bottling took place just two days a week.

New equipment was even bought in the year before closure to increase efficiency, hoping that this, in turn, would boost profits. But this` too failed to produce the increased profits Arkell's was hoping for. The sad decision to close was made and on 1 March 1983, the last bottle came off the production line.

Ironically, this was a bottle of Guinness. All breweries used to bottle their own Guinness at the time.

The bottling equipment was all sold and the former bottling plant is now used for storage. Today, Arkell's beers are bottled on a contract basis.

Work in the bottling plant was considered women's work. At one time it employed over 20 women. At the end, there were five staff remaining. It was a happy place, recalls Don Kenchington, who was Bottling Manager before becoming Head Brewer.

"I remember everybody singing along to the radio as they went about their work," Don remembers.

The bottling store even had its own Christmas parties, separate from the rest of the brewery — a tradition Don started.

Peter Arkell said:"Closing the bottling store was one of the hardest decisions I had to make, but a necessary one.

"It did not make economic sense to keep it open."

Of the bottling staff, three people remain: sisters Carol Mildenhall and Christine Trinder and their nephew, Kevin Gleed.

Kevin is a driver for the Brewery, while Christine and Carol sort out deliveries.

They still work in the former bottling store though, and wouldn't have it any other way.

"It's been like a home to us for the past 40 years," said Christine with a smile. "I can still remember the laughter, fun and happy atmosphere that always existed right to the end. Those memories will never leave me."

CHAPTER EIGHT

"GOOD PUBS, GOOD LANDLORDS"

Stories from behind the bar.

ARKELL'S is not just famous for its fine range of beers; equally as important are its estate of pubs and their licensees.

From the first days of the company, John Arkell set the principle that to enjoy good beer people needed good pubs and good landlords. That tradition continues today, even though the chain of pubs now stretches from Berkshire through Swindon and Cirencester up to Cheltenham and Gloucester.

Although they range from small rural inns to modern town pubs one thing is always the same: the high standard. Arkell's pubs have also moved with the times and today most boast excellent food and many welcome families.

Peter Arkell realised the importance of having good landlords early in his career - in fact before he even came to work for his family firm. After a distinguished war record, he returned to Hammonds of Bradford where he had studied brewing before the war. He ran 30 houses under direct management.

"I learnt a lot in my time at Hammond's which has served me well over the years,"

Peter recalls. "The most important thing was the co-operation and sound advice of the good licensees. I couldn't have managed without it. They were invaluable and became good friends.

"It was also essential - no, vital - to see the licensees were well looked after; something I always fought for. After all, they backed me and I, in turn, backed them: to get their private quarters and licensed houses to standards that reflected their efforts.

"I learnt a lot from those experiences, including the fact that a good licensee can sell anything. The personal welcome and atmosphere a host creates sells more products than any amount of advertising."

Arkell's has a knack of selecting excellent licensees - and keeping them. Many stay for decades, some in the same pub, while others move pub but stay within the firm. One is Henry Archer who celebrated 26 years with the Brewery. Henry, who runs The Tavern, Kemble, Gloucestershire, was presented with a solid silver salver by Managing Director James Arkell.

26 years of silver service. From left, Tavern publicans Henry and Jean Archer being presented with a silver salver from Managing Director James Arkell.

His first Arkell's pub was The Golden Cross in Cirencester town centre, where he spent 17 years. He moved to The Tavern in 1984 so he could run a country pub. Henry is the longest-serving publican in the South Gloucestershire area. Only one other Arkell's licensee has spent more years with the firm.

In Swindon the longest serving publicans are Ray and Marlene Cox of The Wheatsheaf Inn, Stratton-St-Margaret. They should have been presented with a silver salver by Chairman Peter Arkell, at the Brewery but since Ray never takes time off and doesn't like leaving the pub, Mr Arkell decided to present

Everything stops for tea... Wheatsheaf licensees Ray and Marlene Cox (centre) at their "suprise" party.

the award at The Wheatsheaf.

Ray said:"I don't take time off to have a social life, because the pub is my social life. Nothing can beat standing behind my bar and talking to people I've known for 25 years and who have become my friends."

Ray, a former car worker, has not taken a day off for the last 15 years. So when regulars decided to give him a party they thought it would be best to hold it in the pub.

One of the party organisers Carole Day said:"We knew Ray doesn't like to leave his pub and never takes time off. So instead of taking him out to a party we thought we would bring a party to the pub."

The Wheatsheaf's customers worked out a rota to go behind the bar while Ray and Marlene, who thought the party was for a regular's 60th birthday, had a night off.

One man who spent even longer behind the bar for Arkell's was Ron Franklin. Before retiring in 1991 Ron, 69, was also one of the longest serving chairmen in the history of Swindon and District Licensed Victuallers' Association (LVA).

Arkell's has always had very close links with the LVA, sponsoring LVA events and supporting it wherever possible. The role of the LVA has changed greatly over the years from an organisation that dealt purely with brewery-tenant issues like rents to one that liaises with the police and community services.

Under his chairmanship, the LVA successfully introduced the I.D. card scheme to combat the problem of under-age drinking in Swindon.Ron's first stint as LVA chairman was in 1980-84. After a two year break he became Vice-Chairman - but only for six months. When the Chairman became ill Ron took over and stayed in the post until 1991. The post is usually held for just two years.

Ron entered the trade after being made redundant from Swindon rail works in 1960. His first pub was the old Carpenters Arms, Cricklade Road, Swindon, now demolished.

Two years later he became manager of the Carpenters Arms, Chapel St, Gorse Hill, which was later renamed the Swiss Chalet. In 1965 he became manager of The Great Western Hotel, opposite Swindon Railway Station and now called the Flag and Whistle, and five years later took over The Plough, which was also given a new name - The Rat Trap - shortly afterwards.

As well as making sure their licensees are the best, Arkell's also invests heavily in refurbishing and updating its pubs. An on-going refurbishment programme means there is always one pub undergoing a

Mother and son Anne and James Arkell celebrate the Boundary House opening.

ARKELLS BREWERY
2 MILES →
LANDS END
← 231 MILES

72

Reaching new heights... Publican John Turner celebrates the Royal Oak's new look with James Arkell.

but today the town's modern Western Development starts from that point. The £250,000 refurbishment brought the pub bang up-to-date with a conservatory and an extended bar. The milestone was officially unveiled by Peter Arkell's wife Anne at a special ceremony.

John Turner, the brewery's longest-serving tenant, was given a new look for his pub, The Royal Oak in Lechlade, where he has been for 31 years.

Arkell's spent over £100,000 refurbishing the pub, but ensuring none of the character was taken from the country hostelry. Among the improvements were: new toilets, including one for the disabled, a new cellar, an extension with a bay window and a longer bar. All traditional materials were used in the renovation to maintain the pub's rural atmosphere.

John, who has never taken a holiday since he took over the pub, was worried he would have to close while the work was carried out. But it was business as usual during the renovations with John serving from a bar in the skittle alley at the back of the pub.

The bay window on the extension brought back memories for John and his wife June. She said Sir Noël Arkell, Peter's father, had often commented on how nice a bay window would look.

Tradition was also important in the renovation of The Dolphin in Rodbourne Road, Swindon. Arkell's gave the £150,000 facelift project to a Bath-based designer whose trademark is using only antique furniture, fittings and recycled materials. Among the items Jean

facelift to bring it up to the high standards demanded by the firm.

Over the past five years the programme has been stepped up a gear as Arkell's has bought pubs in Cheltenham and Gloucester which required changing to bring them into line with Arkell's style. But some of its most popular Swindon pubs have also been rejuvenated through refurbishment.

The Red Lion, at The Street, Moredon, was given a new name - Boundary House - when it was refurbished and, to mark the occasion, a milestone was placed outside the Victorian pub.

The pub was the last in the town before the open countryside to the West of Swindon

George put in the pub were a bar made from parts of two 100-year-old bars, 18th century carved oak furniture and Turkish carpets.

Pride of place went to a 1920s 18-inch gong which replaced the traditional pub bell and is used by managers Malcolm and Paula Holloway to call time.

The Dolphin had literally gone 'green'; even the walls were painted the colour to complete the new look. Managing Director James Arkell gave Ms George a free hand to transform the pub.

The pub's new look was the result of five-and-a-half month's work, much of it spent by Ms George scouring the country for items to furnish The Dolphin.

As well as the antiques, the pub was also brought up-to-date with a new kitchen and toilets, including one for the disabled, and a new patio.

One of Arkell's most popular pubs, The King's Arms, in Swindon's Old Town, was given a facelift in 1993. Again, close attention was paid to the traditional interior of this impressive 19th Century hotel, popular with business people working in nearby offices and journalists from the nearby Evening Advertiser.

Another pub, The Exmouth Arms in Cheltenham, was refurbished - and the official re-opening party turned into a family affair when Viscount Exmouth pulled the first pint. The pub is named after one of Viscount Exmouth's ancestors, a 19th century naval

Kenny Ball swings at the King's with the help of barmaid Denise Bowden.

74

hero, and its sign - a ship on the ocean - is the same as the Viscount's family crest.

The pub underwent extensive refurbishment including a spacious L-shaped bar, a new kitchen and new toilets with facilities for the disabled. But like all Arkell's pubs to get facelifts, The Exmouth lost none of its traditional appeal: its open fireplace, the dartboard and shoveha'penny were all kept.

It was also business as usual while the work was being carried out. Tenant Geoff Ratcliffe and manager John Lerwell served customers from a temporary bar.The St James Hotel in Cheltenham was also given a new look ten months after being taken over by Arkell's. Some £150,000 was spent on the Victorian hotel although this time it was so extensive it had to close.

It was totally rewired and the two bars knocked into one, creating a more open-plan bar. New toilets and a new kitchen were constructed to complete the new look. There was also a new restaurant and the hotel's ten bedrooms were refurbished. The hotel's attractive and distinctive exterior, which has won awards, was retained.

The St James was officially opened by the Deputy Mayor of Cheltenham, Councillor Alexis Cassin who pulled the first pint.

In total, Arkells bought eight former Whitbread-owned pubs, four in Cheltenham, three in Gloucester and one in Cirencester in 1991 as part of a £1m-plus package.But drinkers in these towns found out it was not only the look of the pubs that changed when they were acquired by Arkell's. The beer improved as well.

Acker's no stranger at the Swiss Chalet - seen here with the publicans Pat and Chris Piper.

Managing Director James Arkell said:"Arkell's beers won people over with their distinctive flavour. They had always gone down well with Swindon drinkers and did the same in Cheltenham and Gloucester."

Although a comfortable pub, an excellent pint and a friendly licensee are enough in themselves, some pubs add a fourth element: live music.

The Swiss Chalet in Gorse Hill leads the way in live jazz. Acker Bilk, Kenny Ball and Georgie Fame are among the top names that have appeared there over the past few years. But there are also regular sessions for local bands.

Acker, best known for his hit, "Stranger on the Shore", hadn't performed in a pub since the early days of his career more than 30 years ago. But he appeared at The Swiss

75

Chalet as a favour to his drummer, Richie Bryant.

Richie, Acker's drummer for 20 years, comes originally from Cricklade. He now lives in London, but visits The Swiss Chalet, in Chapel Street, Gorse Hill, on his return visits to the area to see his family.

Swiss Chalet manager Chris Piper asked him if jazz legend Acker would appear at one of the regular Thursday evening jazz sessions. Acker agreed and appeared without the backing of his Paramount Jazz Band but with the M4 Allstars, a band made up of musician friends who live in towns along the motorway, instead.

Kenny Ball also made two rare pub appearances at The Swiss Chalet, returning for the second on the insistence of his friend Richie after Acker's spectacular success at the pub.

For the return gig the M4 Allstars again provided the backing to replace Kenny's famous Jazzmen. And when the recently-refurbished King's Arms in Old Town wanted someone to crown its new look, who better to turn to than Jazz King Kenny?

Another famous face to appear at an Arkell's pub was Emmerdale soap star Amos Brearly - actor Ronald Magill.

Amos swapped The Woolpack in the Yorkshire Dales for The Great Western to collect a cheque for £3,000 towards heart research. Most of the money was raised at the British Beermat Collectors' Society Convention held at the pub shortly before. It attracted collectors from as far away as Australia. Money was also raised by raffle

Emmerdales' Amos pulls a pint for charity.

ticket sales in all Arkell's pubs.

Mr Magill, President of the Society, handed over the cheque to a representative of the British Heart Foundation after a day-long national meeting of the society at the pub. Arkell's offered to host the presentation to give both the Beermat Collectors' Society and charity a boost.

The Bull at Fairford was the scene for non-stop gags when its new licensee took over. TV comedian Duggie Brown, brother of the new licensee Keith Dudley, agreed to do the honours when Keith took over the 15th century hotel, a former coaching house.

Keith also has a famous showbiz sister: Lynne Perrie, Coronation Street's Ivy Tilsley. Although showbusiness runs in his family Keith says he is happiest behind the bar, pulling pints.

He had no experience of the trade until he joined Arkell's. He had previously worked as an engineer in Zambia, where his wife Judy ran a restaurant.

Keith and Judy, like most Arkell's licensees, offer excellent food in their pub. The importance of good quality food was encouraged many years ago by Peter Arkell. Early in his career at Hammonds he saw how even though pub food was a far cry from what it is today it was still importance.

"In a Northern pub the traditional pub grub was sandwiches, crisps, pickled onions, a slice of pork pie and a hunk of bread – a great favourite," he recalls.

But later he realised that the future lay with attracting more women and families into

Black Horse publican Gerry Aubrey celebrates success with CAMRA representatives Ian Drinkwater and Dave Backhouse, right. (see pages 35 and 89).

pubs and putting the old days of the beer-house behind them.

Peter said:"The ladies toilets and family rooms were and are important. If they are right wives, girlfriends and mothers bring the business in and the men and their children with them!".

Non-stop gags at The Bull. Left to right: Hosts Keith and Judy Dudley, Keith's brother TV Comedian Duggie Brown and wife Jackie.

CHAPTER NINE

DAYS OF WINE ...

The story of John Arkell Vintners - the brewery's wine department.

THE SWINGING Sixties was a time of great change for the British public. It proved lucky for Arkell's too, for it was in this climate of change that John Arkell Vintners, the company's wine department, was born.

Arkell's had bought its wines and spirits for several years from the two prominent wine shops in the town: Goddard's in Regent Street and Brown and Plummer's, owned by distant relations of Peter's family, in Swindon's Old Town.

But in May 1962, Peter Arkell decided it was time to act. He knew the time was approaching for the company to buy its wines direct from the distributors.

Spirits had always been a buoyant market and wine, he knew, would be a high-growth market in the years to come. The closure of Goddard's in 1962 brought matters to a head and John Little to Arkell's to help set up John Arkell Vintners.

John had a wealth of experience which proved invaluable to the vintners from the very beginning. He had been wine manager at Goddard's since 1955, having joined the firm in 1948 as second assistant.

When he started at Goddard's, he knew absolutely nothing about wine and hardly anything about spirits, he admits.

"I was thrown in at the deep end on the first night, which I suppose is the best way of learning isn't it? In those days, the business was known as the wine trade, although very little wine was sold. In the late forties and early fifties, cocktails were the in-drink. Damson Creme, Green Goddess, Late Night Final. Martini was just coming in. Whisky, gin and brandy were very popular as they were so reasonably priced. Whisky was just 44 shillings a bottle.

"Only the rich drank wine. Brown and Plummer's sold wine and Goddard's sold the bread and butter such as whisky, gin and other spirits."

In the early 1960s, wine was growing rapidly in popularity. Peter Arkell had the foresight to realise it would become a huge growth market with the increasing interest in dining out.

He remembers:"Arkell's was the first to bring in pub catering.

It all began in the Swinging Sixties. Chairman Peter Arkell with former
John Arkell Vintners Executive Director, John Little.

"I knew that food was the way forward. Pubs had to change; from the traditional ale house that had men only standing at the bar to the sort that women would like to go into. I had a gut feeling that wine would be a growth market in years to come."

And he was proved right. Peter had known John for years because Arkell's had an account with Goddard's to supply their pubs and off-licenses with spirits.

"John had known most of our licensees and had an excellent relationship with them," said Peter. "This was important; it meant that they could trust him to choose the best wines for them to go with their excellent pub food."

Peter had been thinking about setting up a vintners for some time before fate stepped

in and made his dream a reality with the closure of Goddard's. This left John without a job until Peter stepped in with an offer: to set up John Arkell Vintners.

"At the time, Arkell's proved to be a salvation for me," said John. "Peter offered me the job to set up and run the vintners and asked me to go home and think about it: I didn't need to think about it! I rang him and said 'let's have a chat about it.' Of course I wanted the job, needed the job."

John had an appointment to see Sir Noël; Peter's father, his uncle Graham, Arkell's Chairman, and Peter himself.

"He said, 'This is Mr Little. He's here because we are thinking of starting our own wine department.' Graham said, 'We don't know anything about this! What salary do you expect Little?'

"I said 'I won't come here for anything less than £1,000 a year.' Mr. Graham said 'We can't afford that'." John told him he could not work there for less.

"I don't know why I said that because I was desperate and badly needed any job, and a job with Arkell's was like a dream come true and a house came with the job!" said John.

But Peter talked the other directors round and so John started - on what was a very good salary at the time, of £1,000 a year.

John Arkell Vintners was officially formed on May 4 1962 and opened for business in July.

Wine and spirits were bought primarily for Arkell's pubs and a small percentage for the free trade which in the 1960s was within a 15-mile radius of Arkell's Swindon heartland.

Around £20,000 was spent converting the old mineral store at the Brewery to a wine merchants with wine racks, central heating and stock. The work took two months. Choosing the stock was crucial - but it was left entirely to John. "I was cautious in the beginning, but there had to be a varied stock," said John.

John Arkell Vintners only stocked around 30 types of wine, mostly Spanish, when it opened.

John recalls:"Spanish Sauterne was the

Today, John Arkell Vintners carries over 1000 lines of wines.

big thing in the beginning. This was because people had started to go abroad for their holidays to places like Benidorm and the Costa Del Sol. Gin and whisky were the most popular spirits at the time of opening."

John was given a secretary and a storeman/driver Viv Baxter.

An Arkell's beer rep, Reg Westbury, set about drumming up business. John brought a lot of business from his time at Goddard's.

According to Edgar Dash, Arkell's financial director at the time, to break even they had to turnover £60,000. Goddard's turnover in its final year had been around £82,000.In its first month, John Arkell Vintners' takings reached £10,000 and in the first year turnover was more than £140,000 – exceeding even John and Peter's expectations!

Peter was ecstatic! He told John a couple of months later that he had had many sleepless nights worrying about the new venture.

"Peter took a chance by setting up the wine department, the first brewer in the area to have done it, so it was a big risk," said John. "He also took a chance on me. For that I will always be grateful."

The product list in the beginning was only a couple of pages long – hardly recognisable from the 30 page wine list of today. In the beginning, hardly any pubs stocked wine. John remembers going into a pub asking for a glass – they thought he was mad!

Business grew year on year. Five years after opening, John recruited an assistant.

Trade with restaurants began to grow. And then the corporate trade mushroomed in the 1970s when major national and international businesses began to locate their headquarters to Swindon. John Arkell Vintners' trading area spread to 40 miles along the M4 corridor.

John realised he had to keep up with the latest trends to satisfy consumer demand. He gained as much knowledge as he could about wine, becoming a Prevost – a high ranking position among wine professionals in France and the only Prevost in the UK. John was made an executive director in 1970. He retired in 1992.

A new venture... and many sleepless nights!

Today, John Arkell Vintners is run by director Nick Arkell and his team – Carl Thompson and Mary Prior who have both served over 20 years with the company.

Instead of one rep., to cover the whole of John Arkell Vintners' trading area, there are now two - Richard Turner, who is also free trade director, and Keith Cridland.

The team also consists of storeman Dave Smith, whose father Merv helped set up the liason Committee in 1975, and drivers Ray Shirley and James Clarke. Ray has also served over 20 years with the company.

Nick took over in July 1992 – the Vintners' 30th anniversary, but he already had a great deal of experience in the wine trade.His father Deryk Arkell, a second – cousin of Peter's, had owned Brown and Plummer's, which had been in his family for generations. It closed in 1972 after it was bought by Arkell's.

Vintners and Sales Director Nick Arkell has always had wine in his blood.

Nick joined the brewery in 1973 starting in sales and becoming sales director three years later.

"Wine has always been in my blood!" joked Nick.

His earliest memories of wine are of helping in the shop.

"They were wonderful days - helping out. I can still smell the wonderful combinations of different bouquets even now."

When Nick joined, Arkell's free trade was rapidly expanding from a 15 mile to the 40 mile radius it is today. Swindon's rapid expansion as a business centre meant the growth of restaurants and corporate dining rooms and they needed wines as well as spirits.

"Restaurants and corporate dining rooms were just coming on board," he said."Wine outsells spirits by three to one now and is growing further still," said Nick.

Today, John Arkell Vintners supplies free houses, restaurants, corporate dining rooms as well as its private customers and Arkell's-owned pubs and clubs with quality wines and spirits.

Nick has made sure budget-priced wines

Boxing clever – the John Arkell Vintners team. Left to right: Nick Arkell, Roger Prior, Dave Smith, Mary Prior, Carl Thompson and James Clarke.

are stocked to compete in the fiercely competitive marketplace – but won't sacrifice the Vintners' high quality standards. But he ensures that the tradition intrinsic to the firm stays alive.

"Service and help is what people first came to us for and that is still what they expect," said Nick.

Unlike John, who solely managed the Vintners, Nick ensures he is still involved with sales, but makes sure that Carl and Mary are totally involved.

"We are a team. Teamwork is the only way forward," he said.

The Vintners was recently extended and is now double the size it was in 1962. Around £60,000 was spent on the refurbishment, showing the level of commitment.

"We can carry more stock, more variety and keep prices down," explained Nick.

The John Arkell Vintners of today carries all sorts of wine from all over the world - the New World, Australian, Californian to Chilean – as well as a range from France, Germany and Italy that is second-to-none. Today, there are over 1,000 lines of wines – a far cry from the 30 types of wine in 1962.

"Foreign travel is commonplace and people have become more experimental as time has gone on," said Nick.

The company now also does direct deliveries locally. Also with every bottle of wine bought from Arkell's comes a complete service of advice and information – that little bit extra. It's this that sets it apart from other wine suppliers.

"We are well respected by the trade but we would very much like to encourage ordinary wine drinkers to feel they can come in to buy our wine," said Nick.

Nick or Carl will be happy to advise – even for a single bottle. John Arkell Vintners plans

What a lotta bottle! Don Kenchington at a Vintners wine tasting.

to expand its business supplying weddings - which includes free hire of glasses - and its links with the trade are also being strengthened. It has held annual trade fairs since 1979.

Wine tastings are also held twice a year where private, corporate and trade customers are invited to try the latest wines on offer from all over the world – a far cry from the Spanish Sauterne of 30 years ago and John Arkell Vintners' humble beginnings.

But despite this rapid growth the company has not forgotten the standards it set out to achieve in the beginning.

Johm arkell Vintners assistant Mary Prior and boilerhouse worker Mick Henley celebrate a total of 40 years with the company.

JOHN ARKELL VINTNERS
TOP TIPS

On red, rose and sparkling wines never keep them chilled all day long - an hour at the most is all that's needed.

ON WHITES ...
Chilling for too long will hide all the flavour and bouquet of the wine.

ON REDS ...
Try and decant the wine if at all possible it REALLY makes a difference and brings out the best in any wine.

ON FORTIFIED WINES ...
Serve port and darker sherries at room temperature; pale sherries are best served chilled.

ON STORAGE ...
Reds and whites stay their best if stored at a temp of 55° F.

Port should be stored away from direct light and in a draught free cellar.

ON GLASSES ...
Never fill a wine glass more than two thirds full. This will leave room in the glass for the bouquet as well as the wine and will show people you are a real wine connoisseur!

CHAPTER TEN

ANNIVERSARY YEAR - 1993

A celebration of 150 years of brewing.

THE ANNIVERSARY YEAR of 1993 was a milestone in the Brewery's history. It gave the company, its staff and Arkell's beer drinkers everywhere a chance to look back over the Brewery's past successes - and look ahead to the future.

People needed cheering up. The country was still in the worst recession in living memory. Unemployment was high and morale was lowIn the midst of all this Arkell's celebrated 150 years in brewing - and gave people a chance to cheer up! Chairman Peter Arkell was determined to make the year a memorable one for everyone. And what a year it was!

He recalls:"I wanted our anniversary year to be a year to remember. After all, one hundred and fiftieth anniversaries don't come round in everyone's lifetime!"

Events were planned throughout the year to make sure the anniversary stayed uppermost in the minds of Arkell's workers and drinkers. From the unveiling of a special plaque to the launch of a new beer; a garden party to an open day, hardly a week went by without a special event.

Work had started on the celebrations 1? months before and painstaking plans had been made to ensure everything went off without a hitch. To kick off the year of events, the flag that had flown for years outside the Brewery wa taken down and a new one raised in the anniversary colours of gold and black.

Three generations of Arkells Peter, James and his eldest son George 14, watched proudly as the flag was raised by former Head Brewer Don Kenchington, to the accompaniment of a pair of Roya Yeomanry trumpeters.

Don, who had retired the previous year had been asked to supervise the flag raising A spell in the Navy had shown him the rope and the old flag was taken down without muck effort and the new one raised amid muck cheering.

Managing Director James Arkell then

Three generations of Arkell's raise the Anniversary Flag. Left to right: Peter, James and George.

announced the programme of events for the year as the anniversary flag flew proudly above the Brewery.

After the ceremony there was a party in the cellar bar for staff and directors, including former directors: John Little, Executive Director of John Arkell Vintners; former Financial Director, Edgar Dash and former Tied Trade Director, Ron Siddall.

Company Secretary Teresa Hill remembers:"I'll never forget the magic of that day and the look on everyone's faces! I felt so proud to be part of a company that had survived 150 years."

In fact, not one but four anniversary flags were specially produced for that year; the elements would take their toll on them, wearing out the fabric.

In March, Arkell's Anniversary Ale (3A), made its debut at a tasting - two weeks before it was made available in selected Arkell's

pubs. The beer was a strictly limited edition. Only 8,000 bottles, in 2,000 commemorative four-packs, were produced. Arkell's shareholders and employees received some packs - which were in the anniversary colours of gold and black - while others packs were presented at official functions throughout the year.

Dave Backhouse, Chairman of CAMRA's Swindon Branch, was presented with the first four bottles in their special commemorative pack at the 3A launch at the Brewery.

Also present were Bill Carling, General Secretary of the Brewer's Guild and father of rugby star Will Carling. They were joined by Lawrie Stevens, brewery liaison officer of the Labologists Society who received the first label for its extensive archives. The Society collects beer labels from all over the country and has added the Arkell's Anniversary Ale label to its collection.

Because this is a special beer, a Society

Celebrating at the 3A launch: (Left to right) Bill Carling, James Arkell, Don Bracher and Dave Backhouse.

official was invited.

Chairman Peter Arkell said: "Dave Backhouse and Swindon CAMRA have always supported Arkell's and our real ales. That's why he was the obvious choice to get the first taste of this very special beer and be presented with the first four-pack."

The beer with its dark, golden colour and hoppy flavour was a big hit with customers and even more so when it was launched on draught in September.

Head Brewer Don Bracher formulated the recipe with former Head Brewer Don Kenchington; literally a combination of old and new.

Dave Backhouse was to become a regular figure at special events throughout anniver-

Arkell's Anniversary Ale (3A) – a strictly limited edition.

sary year; showing the close links between Arkell's and CAMRA.

In the summer CAMRA bestowed a major honour on Arkell's when The Black Horse at Wanborough won through to the finals of its National Pub of the Year contest. Regulars were served beer at 5p a pint all evening to celebrate.

The Black Horse was the first Arkell's pub to win the Campaign for Real Ale regional pub of the year. Licensee Gerry Aubrey was presented with a special certificate by CAMRA - and immediately knocked the price of 2B down from £1.32 to just 5p a pint for the evening.

Gerry's father Stan had run the pub for 21 years before Gerry took over 15 years ago. Gerry decided to take the price of a pint 36 years ago - roughly two shillings or 10p - and halve it. Gerry said his father would have been proud that the pub and the condition of its beer had beaten hundreds of others across seven counties from Buckinghamshire to the Isle of Wight to win the award.

Handing over the award, CAMRA President Ian Drinkwater said classic inns like The Black Horse were fast disappearing, being destroyed by 'theme pubs'. He said it was important the heritage of the traditional British pub remained. The contest was held to make sure that happened.

The Black Horse was nominated by the Swindon CAMRA Branch for its beer, hospitality and general atmosphere as well as the friendliness of its host. The award echoed founder John Arkell's motto 'Good beers, good pubs, good landlords' 150 years on. The

Winning team: The Lidens' John Honeyman and Karen Smith.

pub's feat came during the first British Pub Week between June 28 and July 4 which was set up to mark the contribution pubs like Arkell's ones make to the community.

Arkell's licensees John Honeyman and Karen Smith kicked off British Pub Week by handing over the running of their pub, The Liden Arms, for the day.

Housewife Sue Taylor, 34, and storeman Nick Hindmarsh, 31, were the winners of a raffle staged by the pub to launch the week of special events in Arkell's pubs.

John dreamed up the idea of the raffle to show people what it was really like to run a pub. Sue and Nick soon found it was not as easy as most people think. Sue had been a barmaid at The Liden years ago so knew what to do, but Nick had only been on the drinkers' side of the bar and had never pulled a pint in his life.

Their day in charge started at 8am when they let the cleaners in and sorted out the tills.

Passport to prizes

They then had to make the bar snacks and prepare vegetables for the roast lunches while also bottling up and making sure the pressure on the beer pumps was correct. And that was before they even let the first customer in.

Arkell's staged a host of other events for Pub Week including an electronic golf evening, a Mr and Miss Moonraker and a Mr and Mrs competition at The Moonrakers pub. The Swindon Morris Men performed at The Sun Inn at Coate and The White Hart at Stratton.

The Brewery also held a competition for the best dressed managed house with a day at the races for the winning couple: John and Karen from The Liden.

Arkell's extended its estate during the anniversary year by buying the freehold of the former British Legion Club in Havelock Street, Swindon.

The club, which had lost its affiliation to the Royal British Legion prior to the acquisition, was renamed the Havelock Street Combined Services Club - although Arkell's promised business as usual for members.

James Arkell said:"We were delighted to acquire the property. It was a shame that the British Legion's affiliation was lost. However,

it was the Brewery's intention to provide a club of equally good reputation for its members."

Another high point of the year for real ale fans was the Passport Promotion. Special Arkell's Anniversary Passports were available in all its pubs offering the chance to win commemorative prizes.

Hundreds of passport holders claimed prizes by simply buying a drink at a set number of Arkell's pubs. After visiting 70 of Arkell's 82 pubs and off-licences, the Anniversary Passport holder could claim a specially engraved pewter tankard and an anniversary tie. Women could have a make-up compact and wine goblet if they preferred.

There was also a prize of a special edition four-pack of Arkell's Anniversary Ale (3A) and a certificate for those who visited all 82. The first and 150th passport holders completing the first stage also won a tour of the Brewery.

Peter Arkell said:"We wanted to give people who enjoy our beer a fun way of helping us to celebrate our 150th anniversary. Everyone has their own favourite Arkell's pub and each one has its own unique character. The Anniversary Passport has given people the opportunity to go and visit them all and collect some special souvenirs at the end of their tour around Arkell's country."

Passport to prizes: first passport winner Chris Smith (centre) with his prizes
and Peter Arkell (left) and James Arkell (right).

The first winner was pilot Chris Smith who proved he was a real high flier - by completing it in just four-and-a-half days. Chris, 43, of Grange Park, Swindon, who works for Virgin Atlantic, was presented with his prizes by Peter Arkell at his local The Wild Deer, in Westcott Place, Swindon.

Chris had some time to kill and decided to complete the Anniversary Passport while he renovated his 13-year-old MGB car. He had to drive 1,000 miles to run in the rebuilt engine - and completing the passport was the best way.

He clocked up around 440 miles travelling to Arkell's pubs in Newbury, Cheltenham and Gloucester as well as those nearer home. He drank his favourite tipple, Arkell's 3B, when he wasn't driving - but for those further afield he stuck to soft drinks, since the passport allows non-alcoholic drinks for drivers.

His tankard replaced one he was awarded ten years ago when Arkell's ran a similar promotion. Chris took nine days to complete that promotion - even though Arkell's had 20 fewer pubs. But even his effort this time was beaten by an Arkell's licensee and nine of his regulars.

They travelled 334 miles in a day visiting all 82 pubs and off-licenses. The pub crawl to end all pub crawls was for charity. Ted Cade of The George, Kempsford, and his team raised more than £3,000 to buy and train a

Rising to the challenge – The Arkell's pub challenge team.

guide dog for the blind. It was given an appropriate name - Arkell.

The team drank soft drinks only outside normal opening hours but sunk 41 pints between them in the course of the day. They planned the route with help from Dave Paginton, an Arkell's drayman who knew his way around the pubs.

The team left The George at 7am and was seen off by Peter and Anne Arkell. Many licensees had already raised money for the team through sponsorship while others donated money. At each pub the team had barely time to pass around collecting buckets and finish their drinks before dashing off to the next stop.

Other fans of Arkell's beer took it at a gentler pace. Robert Brailsford even toured all the pubs on his bike.

The distinctive anniversary logo was made into a plaque for the Brewery during the year and was unveiled by the Lord Lieutenant of Wiltshire, Field Marshall Sir Roland Gibbs - almost 150 years to the day that the first pint was brewed.

Trumpeters from the Royal Yeomanry played a fanfare while Sir Roland unveiled the anniversary plaque. After the ceremony Sir Roland and Lady Gibbs met the staff, their families and retired employees.

During the Anniversary year Arkell's came in for many tributes but none as unusual or unexpected as the one on stage at Swindon's Wyvern Theatre.

During a charity show for Swindon's Prospect Foundation hospice appeal, sponsored for the third year by Arkell's, four of the Brewery's own licensees marched on stage carrying their pub signs during the opening number. They then joined in a musical tribute to the firm.

The organisers wanted to pay tribute to the Brewery so sprung the surprise to the delight of Chairman Peter Arkell. He was unaware the special number - part of a selection from Hello Dolly performed by the popular Swindon choir Kentwood - was in the show until choir members started to wave Arkell's anniversary bunting. Trays of Arkell's Anniversary Ale were brought on stage and the four publicans marched on carrying replica pubs signs.

Mr Arkell thought the four publicans: Ron Hare of The Jolly Tar, Dave Selwood of The Fox and Hounds, Liz Bailey of The Freke Arms and Tina Tidy of The Crown, were in their pubs serving customers.

Peter Arkell was also caught unawares at the firm's annual dance for all Brewery staff and licensees in February. All the staff clubbed together to buy him an engraved silver tankard and surprised him by presenting it during the event.

Arkell's brewed another commemorative

Lord Lieutenant Sir Roland Gibbs unveils the anniversary plaque in the prescence of Chairman Peter Arkell.

93

Proud to be part of it all –
Company Secretary Teresa Hill
at the Brewery's Anniversary Open Day.

in traditional RAF blue. For every can sold, Arkell's donated 3p to the RAF Benevolent Fund.

Arkell's already had a long association with the International Air Tattoo and the RAF Benevolent Fund. The company has supplied beer and wines to caterers to airshows for several years.

The RAF Benevolent Fund approached the company to quote for a special beer to mark the Air Force's 75th anniversary. The brief was that the can must be in the RAF colours of blue with red and white and carry the name RAF Anniversary Ale.

Arkell's wasn't the only brewer approached. The company was in competition with two others, one a major national the other a regional brewer. Arkell's had just three months to come up with the recipe for the beer and can design.

The company drafted in Gloucestershire-based Nailsworth Design Company which produced the distinctive design of an eagle flying through a circle with the RAF logo and the motto 'braced by wire to fly by wire'.

Chairman Peter Arkell, who was a pilot during the War, told the press at the Ale's launch:"RAF Anniversary Ale is a real high flier!"

In September the company launched Arkell's Anniversary Ale on draught. It coincided with an open day at the Brewery; the first time it had opened its doors to the public in its 150-year history.

More than 1,500 people flooded through the gates to see for themselves the timeless magic of the Victorian Brewery. Tickets at £2

ale during the year in addition to its Anniversary Ale, although this one was to celebrate another anniversary, that of the RAF.

The company beat off stiff competition to win the contract for the RAF Anniversary Ale and produced almost 100,000 cans of the beer. It was available in cans in pubs, off-licenses, wholesalers and certain supermarkets throughout the UK. NAAFI Clubs also stocked the cans and the beer was made available to RAF bases nationwide.

Arkell's Free Trade Director Richard Turner said:"We were delighted with our RAF Anniversary Ale and proud to be producing it because of our 150th anniversary."

The ale had a distinctive malty flavour with an abv (alcohol by volume) of five per cent. The can had an up-to-the minute design

94

a head sold very fast in the weeks before the event. For most visitors the high point was a tour of the Brewery, giving a rare glimpse into Arkell's traditional brewing process. Naturally there was a chance to sample the finished product in the Brewery cellar bar.

There was also a unique display of Arkell's memorabilia, including beer labels from the past and old pub photos. Other attractions included displays by Swindon Morris Men, Swindon Young Musicians, a barbecue, an Aunt Sally and a bouncy castle.

Anne and Peter Arkell celebrating a bygone age and toasting the future.

Staff were dressed in Victorian costume, reflecting the atmosphere of 1843. Peter Arkell was dressed as his great-grandfather John Arkell, complete with sideburns and his great-grandfather's original tankard.

He looked so like his ancestor, one visitor commented:"It's like going back in time. The Brewery has always looked Victorian and now the staff do too!"

Peter's wife, Anne, completed the look by dressing as a Victorian lady.

Each visitor received a free Arkell's pint or a glass of wine or soft drink and a commemorative pint glass to take home. Children received an anniversary mug. Hundreds of visitors also bought anniversary memorabilia such as T-shirts, posters, key rings, trays, dripmats and even notebooks!

Ian Peaty of the Brewers' History Society travelled from Essex to attend and present Peter Arkell with a special certificate to mark the company's Anniversary Open Day and 150 years in brewing.

Managing Director James Arkell helped serve the drinks at the bar and wash up - he was pleased the Brewery had a glasswasher - while his eldest son George, 14, assisted with the pony rides.

Peter Arkell said:"Our anniversary year certainly lived up to expectations. It will be a hard act to follow when the Brewery's 200th anniversary comes around!"

PUBS IN SWINDON

THE BAKERS ARMS
Beechcroft Road, Upper Stratton,
Swindon
Telephone 0793 832227

THE BAKERS ARMS
16 Emlyn Square, Swindon
Telephone 0793 535199

THE BOUNDARY HOUSE
1 The Street, Moredon, Swindon
Telephone 0793 534186

THE CLIFTON HOTEL
Clifton Street, Swindon
Telephone 0793 523162

THE COUNTY GROUND
115 County Road, Swindon
Telephone 0793 522093

THE CROWN
73 Ermin Street, Stratton St Margaret,
Swindon
Telephone 0793 827530

THE DOLPHIN HOTEL
Rodbourne Road, Swindon
Telephone 0793 523844

THE DUKE OF EDINBURGH
Cricklade Road, Swindon
Telephone 0793 523643

THE DUKE OF WELLINGTON
Eastcott Hill, Swindon
Telephone 0793 534180

THE FLAG AND WHISTLE
Station Road, Swindon
Telephone 0793 522047

THE KINGS ARMS HOTEL
20 Wood Street, Swindon
Telephone 0793 522156

THE KINGSDOWN INN
Kingsdown Road, Upper Stratton,
Swindon
Telephone 0793 824802

THE LAMB AND FLAG
Bridge Street, Swindon
Telephone 0793 536375

THE LIDEN ARMS
Barrington Close, Liden, Swindon
Telephone 0793 522800

LONGS BAR
86/87 Victoria Road, Swindon

Telephone 0793 534519

THE MOONRAKERS
Cricklade Road, Swindon
Telephone 0793 721017

THE NEW INN
Swindon Road, Stratton St Margaret,
Swindon Telephone 0793 822081

THE PLOUGH INN
26 Devizes Road, Swindon
Telephone 0793 535603

THE RAT TRAP
Highworth Road, Stratton St Margaret,
Swindon
Telephone 0793 823282

THE RUNNING HORSE
Wootton Bassett Road, Swindon
Telephone 0793 523903

THE STEAM TRAIN
Cheney Manor Road, Rodbourne,
Swindon
Telephone 0793 535318

THE SUN INN
Coate, Swindon
Telephone 0793 523292

THE SWISS CHALET
Chapel Street, Swindon
Telephone 0793 535610

THE WHEATSHEAF INN
Ermin Street, Stratton St Margaret
Telephone 0793 823149

THE WHITE HART
Oxford Road, Stratton, Swindon
Telephone 0793 822272

THE WILD DEER
Westcott Place, Swindon
Telephone 0793 523238

THE OFF-LICENCE
373 Cricklade Road, Swindon
Telephone 0793 523508
THE OFF-LICENCE
Prospect Place, Swindon
Telephone 0793 512752
THE OFF-LICENCE
60 Rodbourne Road, Swindon
Telephone 0793 521224

PUBS OUTSIDE SWINDON
THE ADAM AND EVE
8, Townsend Street, Cheltenham, Gloucestershire.
Telephone 0242 525452
THE ANGEL
High Street, Purton, Swindon, Wiltshire.
Telephone 0793 770248
THE BAKERS ARMS
Badbury, Swindon, Wiltshire.
Telephone 0793 740313
THE BAKERS ARMS
Ferndale Street, Faringdon, Oxon.
Telephone 0367 240574
THE BEAR HOTEL
1 High Street, Marlborough, Wiltshire.
Telephone 0672 512134
THE BELL INN
Purton Stoke, Swindon, Wiltshire.
Telephone 0793 770434
THE BLACK HORSE
Upper Wanborough, Swindon, Wiltshire.
Telephone 0793 790305
THE BOROUGH ARMS
High Street, Wootton Bassett, Swindon, Wiltshire.
Telephone 0793 854833
THE BREWERS ARMS
70 Cricklade Street, Cirencester, Gloucestershire.
Telephone 0285 653763
THE BREWERS ARMS
High Street, Wanborough, Swindon, Wiltshire.
Telephone 0793 790707
THE BULL HOTEL
Market Place, Fairford, Gloucestershire.
Telephone 0285 712535
THE BUTCHERS ARMS
26 Greatfield, Nr Swindon, Wiltshire.
Telephone 0793 770726

THE CARPENTERS ARMS
South Marston, Swindon, Wiltshire.
Telephone 0793 823179
THE COOPERS ARMS
Bartholomew Street, Newbury, Berkshire.
Telephone 0635 47469
THE CROWN INN
Broad Hinton, Nr Swindon, Wiltshire.
Telephone 0793 731302
THE CURRIERS ARMS
High Street, Wootton Bassett, Swindon, Wiltshire.
Telephone 0793 854814

THE DUKE OF EDINBURGH
Woodside Road, Winkfield, Nr Windsor, Berkshire.
Telephone 0344 882 736
THE DUKE HOTEL
Hilmarton, Nr Calne, Wiltshire.
Telephone 024 976 634
THE EIGHT BELLS
East End, Fairford, Gloucestershire.
Telephone 0285 712369
THE EXMOUTH ARMS
Bath Road, Cheltenham, Gloucestershire.
Telephone 0242 528149
THE FOX AND HOUNDS
Markham Road, Wroughton, Swindon, Wiltshire.
Telephone 0793 812217
THE FOX INN
Swindon Street, Highworth, Swindon, Wiltshire.
Telephone 0793 762313
THE FREKE ARMS
Swanborough, Hannington, Swindon, Wiltshire.
Telephone 0793 762297
THE GEORGE
Kempsford, Fairford, Gloucestershire.
Telephone 0285 810236

97

THE GEORGE HOTEL
High Street, Lambourn, Berkshire.
Telephone 0488 71889

THE GOLDEN CROSS
Blackjack Street, Cirencester, Gloucestershire.
Telephone 0285 652137

THE HEREFORD ARMS
Winchcombe Street, Cheltenham, Gloucestershire.
Telephone 0242 221401

THE HIGHWAYMAN INN
Beech Pike, Elkstone, Nr Cheltenham,
Gloucestershire. Telephone 0285 821221

THE INDIA HOUSE
227, Barton Street, Gloucester, Gloucestershire.
Telephone 0452 413218

THE JOLLY TAR
Queens Road, Hannington, Swindon, Wiltshire.
Telephone 0793 762245

THE LORD LYON
Stockcross, Newbury, Berkshire.
Telephone 0488 38366

THE OLD BEAR
High Street, Cricklade, Wiltshire.
Telephone 0793 750005

YE OLDE RED LION
Green Lane, Chieveley, Newbury, Berkshire.
Telephone 0635 248379

THE PLOUGH INN
Gloucester Road, Stratton, Cirencester, Gloucestershire
Telephone 0285 653422

THE PLOUGH INN
Lechlade Road, Highworth, Swindon, Wiltshire.
Telephone 0793 762224

THE PLOUGH INN
London Street, Fairford, Gloucestershire.
Telephone 0285 712409

THE PLOUGH INN
Marlborough Road, Badbury, Swindon, Wiltshire.
Telephone 0793 740342

THE PLUME OF FEATHERS
Watermoor Road, Cirencester, Gloucestershire.
Telephone 0285 652112

THE RED LION
High Street, Lechlade, Gloucestershire.
Telephone 0367 252373

THE ROYAL OAK
Bishopstone, Swindon, Wiltshire.
Telephone 0793 790481

THE ROYAL OAK
Oak Street, Lechlade, Gloucestershire.
Telephone 0367 252261

THE SAINT JAMES HOTEL
Ambrose Street, Cheltenham, Gloucestershire.
Telephone 0242 522860

THE SALLY PUSSEY INN
Swindon Road, Wootton Bassett, Swindon, Wiltshire.
Telephone 0793 852430

THE SARACENS HEAD HOTEL
High Street, Highworth, Swindon. Wiltshire.
Telephone 0793 762284

THE SIR COLIN CAMPBELL
Llanthony Road, Gloucester, Gloucestershire.
Telephone 0452 29615

THE TALBOT INN
Victoria Road, Cirencester, Gloucestershire.
Telephone 0285 653760

THE TAVERN INN
Kemble, Cirencester, Gloucestershire.
Telephone 0285 770216

THE THAMES HEAD
Tetbury Road, Cirencester, Gloucestershire.
Telephone 0285 770259

THE THREE TUNS
Devizes Road, Wroughton, Swindon, Wiltshire.
Telephone 0793 812210

THE VICTORIA
Eastleach, Nr Cirencester, Gloucestershire.
Telephone 036 785 277

THE WOODSHAW INN
Garraways, Woodshaw, Wootton Bassett,
Swindon, Wiltshire.
Telephone 0793 854617

THE WHITE HART HOTEL
High Street, Cricklade, Wiltshire.
Telephone 0793 750206

THE WHITESMITH'S ARMS
Southgate Street, Gloucester, Gloucestershire.
Telephone 0452 414770

The author has made every effort to ensure that the factual content is accurate, but cannot be held responsible for any errors or inaccuracies in the information supplied to her.